"Debra White Smith has written a must-read for all lovers of the church—big or small. It is deeply biblical, solidly practical, and eminently relatable. Debra is a tour de force in leading and growing a small church. In this book, she leads the reader to fully understand how a small church can thrive in the present culture of consumerism. She draws on Scripture that speaks perfectly to growing a small church, with practical insights and ideas based on years of ministry in small churches. Her writing is vivid and succinct, with splashes of real-life church humor. This book is remarkable and will become the road map for small-church leaders. If you serve in a small church, or if you serve small-church pastors, this book is required reading. Read it and learn from one of the best!"

—Donna Kyzer-Rice
Public School Administrator
National Motivational Speaker
Small-Church Lay Leader

"If you have the privilege to be around Dr. Smith—as I have for eight years—you would soon hear her heart for the small church. She has a passion for the churches who feel they are too small to be significant. She has focused on projects to assist every church who believes that all the myths of a small church are, in fact, untrue. Her desire is to let each pastor in the harvest field, no matter where his or her call is, have a significant impact on the work of the kingdom. This book provides a perfect snapshot and discussion of the "small-church mentality" that at times has crippled churches in believing they cannot have influence in their communities. This book dispels the myths that often paralyze the church and addresses the reason this myth thinking has invaded the church. Dr. Smith's words also bring hope to the church, along with important steps to becoming the church God wants you to be. Her encouragement is to be who you are and to adopt the strong belief that you *can* be significant if you embrace your call where you are serving out your call. You will find encouragement, inspiration, and challenges on the pages of this book."

—Dr. Keven J. Wentworth
District Superintendent
North/East Texas District
Church of the Nazarene

"In *Small Church, Big Impact*, the spotlight turns, with much-needed acuity, to the myriad of small churches that represent the heart of spirituality across North America. Packed with astute observations and tailored strategies, this book is a seminal guide for pastors and lay leaders committed to nurturing their congregations amid the challenges of our times. With the backdrop of alarming statistics—revealing a significant attendance decline within churches, particularly during the pandemic—this work provides more than mere analysis; it offers hope, practical advice, and a call to action."

—Robert Beckett
Pastor, Author, President of the Revitalization Network

"Dr. Debra White Smith is perfectly qualified to write about leading and growing a small church. As a prolific writer with past and current pastoral experience, Pastor White Smith offers a powerful challenge to pastors. Her seminars and writing are informed by her colorful years of pastoral experience and keen understanding of the challenges small congregations experience in a consumeristic society."

—Dr. David Downs
District Superintendent
West Texas District
Church of the Nazarene

"The opening chapter in this volume exposes the greatest shortcoming for pastors and laity of small churches. The temptation to ignore the incredibly powerful ministries and influence of the small church is the greatest contribution to small churches dying and closing. Debra White Smith's focus on the greater impact inherent in small-church ministry will enlighten and recharge any small-church leader, if he or she only takes it to heart. Having a proper perspective and balance of ministry and relationships in the church is key to impacting individuals and emerging leaders to *be* the church capable of impacting their community and even the world. This work is full of good, solid theology and solid perspectives on ministry and relationships that truly work. Having pastored small churches myself, I highly recommend this book to all small-church pastors and congregations who struggle with a sense of being insignificant in the kingdom. I wish I had known and understood these concepts many years ago."

—Pastor Don Gardner
Palestine Church of the Nazarene, Palestine, Texas
District Superintendent Emeritus, Church of the Nazarene
African Field Director Emeritus, Church of the Nazarene

"*Small Church, Big Impact* is a great resource to help encourage the church community. It has vital information to help guide the church to its purpose in a lost and unchurched community. The author reminds small churches that they are not in competition with other churches of any size, because every church headed by God is an equally important part of his plan for his overall church. This book can be an asset to all churches today because we live in such a competitive world."

—Pastor Marlene James
Bruton Terrace Church of the Nazarene
Dallas, Texas

"The concepts in this book were a great start to my personal rejuvenation as a pastor and the rejuvenation of my church. We began to celebrate our smallness and use it rather than being squeezed by both the church culture and the secular culture. Her passage on entire sanctification is spot-on. Thanks! We as a church are striving to evangelize for the kingdom's sake and not for our own church's sake. Thanks for the jump start!"

—Pastor Randy Larpenteur
Mineola Church of the Nazarene
Mineola, Texas

"OK, I admit it. My view of kingdom success has been tied for too long to the 'bigger is better' mindset. Debra White Smith challenges the origin of the consumer mindset that has produced a generation of church shoppers who expect to be served rather than serve. Consequently, consumers don't bond; they bail.

"Debra has produced an engrossing book every small-church pastor should read. A must-read for any who still believe the small church is 'a problem to be fixed' and not 'an essential element in a divine strategy.'

"I highly recommend her insightful book that calls for a redefinition of pastoral success. The reader will find it anecdotal, principled, practical, openhearted, and enjoyable. Debra's writing voice is so engaging and approachable. My favorite acronym is 'BATS.'"

—Dr. David F. Nixon
District Superintendent Emeritus
Southern Florida District
Church of the Nazarene

"Debra White Smith offers a powerful and helpful encouraging text, *Small Church, Big Impact*. Coming from both a place of ministry experience and passion, Smith offers both a practical and prophetic invitation to guide the flourishing of small churches. It is very easy with a consumeristic mentality to dismiss the importance of smaller churches, yet this is a kingdom mistake. The size of a church cannot be used to measure a local church's faithfulness and kingdom impact. Moreover, in many denominations, churches under one hundred and even under fifty represent the largest number of local churches of any size. Even with this reality, many resources tend to overlook and dismiss teaching and resourcing pastors and congregations for these unique contextual ministries. This resource is specifically focused on pastors and leaders of smaller churches to equip, empower, and encourage.

"This text is honest about common challenges but also invites readers into a new imagination of hope and encouragement about the blessings and advantages of numerically smaller churches. Specifically, the challenge of consumerism can become a heavy millstone around the necks of small-church pastors and leaders when they are unable to match all the products and services that larger churches provide. This text offers both practical and theological wisdom. Churches of all sizes face the challenges of living in a consumer culture. While the specific focus on small churches is evident, pastors leading churches of all sizes will benefit from this gracious and encouraging wisdom. Smith guides all leaders to celebrate the unique gifts and graces that smaller local churches serve in the further inbreaking of God's kingdom over all creation."

—Dr. Brent D. Peterson
Author of *Created to Worship* and two volumes in The Wesleyan Theology Series:
The Church and *The Sacraments*
Dean of the College of Theology and Christian Ministries,
Northwest Nazarene University

"Throughout her book, it becomes clear that Debra White Smith has a deep love for small-church pastors. In a culture where most church leadership books are designed for larger-church pastors, Debra has made a special effort to highlight the advantages as well as the challenges of the small church and provide helpful wisdom for the small-church pastor.

"One of the very best gifts of this book is to help pastors and congregants realize that their struggles are often the result of sociological issues, such as our consumer culture, rather than spiritual issues, such as, 'They're just not committed enough!' She helps us see how this consumer-culture mindset has greatly affected the way we see and do church.

"You will want to read this book to learn how both the pastor and the congregation can get trapped in a 'foster-child syndrome' and how we need to break this. You will also enjoy the metaphor of starting a 'Kangaroo Church'!"

—Dr. Doug Samples
Professor Emeritus, Southern Nazarene University (SNU)
Former Chaplain for the SNU School of Professional and Graduate Studies

"As the sole pastor of a small church, I can say with confidence that Dr. Debra White Smith has hit the nail on the head when she recounts the issues small churches face in a consumer culture. But she doesn't leave it there. Through this book she has provided a practical plan for navigating the landscape and even thriving in it.

"In this book, Dr. Smith provides several ideas for church growth that get our creative juices flowing. But her strategy goes beyond that, touching on the need for prayer and planning to ensure buy-in and executability. She also shares some potential pitfalls and problems that might occur along the way. Her goal is to get congregation members working together to develop a long-term, sustainable plan for outreach to their community—not just numbers in the pew on Sundays, but real and lasting kingdom growth.

"This book is so well organized that it is perfect for referencing back to again and again as a church board and congregation pray about, design, and navigate their own personalized plan for growth and revitalization. I recommend this book to everyone, pastor and layperson alike, who has God's heart for revitalization and growth in the body of Christ."

—Dr. Norita Sieffert, Pastor
Faith Fellowship Church of the Nazarene, Terrell, Texas

"Debra White Smith's book is immensely helpful in considering how the consumer culture impacts the small church. This book is filled with fresh ideas for the church in moving forward and provides laughter at relatable small-church issues. Finally, a pastor who understands the small church! I highly recommend this book to small-church pastors and leadership teams."

—Pastor Kelli Westmark
Lincoln City Church of the Nazarene

SM⛪LL
CHURCH
BIG
IMPACT

Practical Help for Pastoring in a Consumer Culture

Debra White Smith

f⵿

THE FOUNDRY
PUBLISHING®

Copyright © 2025 by Debra White Smith

The Foundry Publishing®
PO Box 419527
Kansas City, MO 64141
thefoundrypublishing.com

ISBN 978-0-8341-4370-8

Cover design: Brandon Hill
Interior design: Sharon Page

Unless otherwise indicated, all Scripture quotations are from the Holy Bible, New International Version® (NIV®). Copyright © 1973, 1978, 1984, 2011 by Biblica, Inc.™ Used by permission of Zondervan. All rights reserved worldwide. www.zondervan.com. The "NIV" and "New International Version" are trademarks registered in the United States Patent and Trademark Office by Biblica, Inc.™

The following version of Scripture is in the public domain:

The King James Version (KJV)

The following copyrighted versions of Scripture are used by permission:

The ESV® Bible (The Holy Bible, English Standard Version®), copyright © 2001 by Crossway, a publishing ministry of Good News Publishers. All rights reserved.

The New American Standard Bible® (NASB®), copyright © 1960, 1962, 1963, 1968, 1971, 1972, 1973, 1975, 1977, 1995 by The Lockman Foundation. www.Lockman.org.

The New King James Version® (NKJV). Copyright © 1982 by Thomas Nelson. All rights reserved.

The Holy Bible, New Living Translation (NLT), copyright 1996, 2004, 2015 by Tyndale House Foundation. Used by permission of Tyndale House Publishers, Carol Stream, IL 60188. All rights reserved.

The Living Bible (TLB), copyright © 1971 by Tyndale House Foundation. Used by permission of Tyndale House Publishers, Carol Stream, Illinois 60188. All rights reserved.

Library of Congress Cataloging-in-Publication Data
A complete catalog record for this book is available from the Library of Congress.

The internet addresses, email addresses, and phone numbers in this book are accurate at the time of publication. They are provided as a resource. The Foundry Publishing® does not endorse them or vouch for their content or permanence.

Dedication

To my dear husband, Daniel W. Smith, who served as copastor with me in the small-church context and supported me through my PhD journey that contributed to the concepts in this book. Thanks for the years of ministry that we have shared as we have learned together and grown together. Thanks also for supporting me through the production of this book.

Special thanks to my church family at Palestine Church of the Nazarene, Palestine, Texas—that zany, endearing bunch of people I have had the honor to pastor and to worship with. While this book is the product of sound, scholarly research, it is also the product of lessons learned while pastoring a small church in North America.

Finally, to my new, "old" church family, Jacksonville First Church of the Nazarene, Jacksonville, Texas. My earliest preschool memories happened in the walls of our church. It's the place I met my husband as a teenager, the place I raised my children in their childhood, and the place I now copastor with my husband. I am looking forward to the future in our new pastoral assignment at Jacksonville First Church as we learn and grow together.

Contents

Foreword

Dr. Debra White Smith thoughtfully helps pastors and lay-people alike to identify the reality of the consumer culture in which we live and how it affects the small church. This book provides meaningful research that will help the small church make a big difference in leading people into a saving relationship with Jesus and in seeing lives and families transformed and, ultimately, whole communities changed.

Dr. Debra White Smith brings not only significant research but also a wealth of experience in pastoring the small church. I have personally relied on Dr. White Smith's understanding of the small church to help form the vision and strategy of our church in the United States and Canada so that it will be applicable and helpful to the thousands of churches in our denomination that are under fifty in worship attendance.

Dr. White Smith's approach throughout this work gives pastors and their leadership teams the opportunity not only to understand key concepts important to the effectiveness of the small church but also to apply them in planning and execution. Don't miss the opportunity at the end of every chapter to encourage, equip, empower, and engage your team through planning the work. I'm thrilled that you have begun reading this exciting book and hope that you will obtain copies for others with whom you can dream, pray, collaborate, and work.

The Lord bless you in this exciting endeavor of partnering with God's grand purpose to see his "kingdom come" and his "will be done, on earth as it is in heaven" (Matt. 6:10). There is no doubt in my mind that the small church is central and essential in his plan!

Read on! Collaborate! Make plans! Do the work and experience the joy of the Lord's harvest!

—Stanley W. Reeder
Regional Director for USA/Canada
Church of the Nazarene

Preface

In this book, I use statistics several times from my denomination, the Church of the Nazarene, and my research indicates that those statistics are reflective of statistics across denominational lines. If you are a member of another denomination, I encourage you to seek out the statistics from your denomination's home office as you journey forward to recognize the value of the small church in the world at large.

Currently, in the Church of the Nazarene, 82 percent of North American churches average ninety-nine or fewer in attendance, and 60 percent average fifty or fewer.[1] According to Dr. Stan Reeder, regional director for the United States and Canada, the average church size in the Church of the Nazarene is forty-nine in attendance.[2] Dr. Reeder further states that the United States and Canada region has seen an approximate 30 percent decrease in attendance in the past seventeen years, with approximately 8 to 15 percent of that decrease occurring during the COVID-19 pandemic.[3] As already indicated, these statistics are not limited to the Church of the Nazarene; they are reflective of a North American trend.[4, 5]

Statistics also point to the reality that there are exponentially more small churches than large churches across denominational lines.[6] Nevertheless, many church growth books, curriculum, and conferences present concepts that work in a larger church but do not translate to the smaller church, leaving a significant gap in the education of small-church pastors across denominational lines. In my study on the topic, published in *Pastoral Psychology*, I found that the lack of training specific to small churches in the consumer culture and the task of managing volunteers can even be linked to burnout.[7] Therefore, the availability of books and curriculum that teach pastors and lay leaders about the challenges faced in the small-church setting and how to overcome those challenges is necessary for the future success of small churches as well as the pastors and lay leaders who serve them. My desire is for this book to be such a resource, and my hope is that small-church pastors and lay leaders in many denominations will find practical, doable concepts for their small churches that will encourage and inspire.

You will see that at the end of each chapter there is a section titled "Pausing to Plan." This section contains key questions and prompts to assist in engaging pastors and lay leaders in collaboration as you think together about ways you can implement the concepts from this book. (For more details, see the end of chap. 1.) Once your plan is complete, the idea is to implement the plan together (see the book's afterword). Thus, the foundational premise of this book is to equip not only small-church pastors but also small-church lay leaders to invest the time together to lay a foundational plan that will guide your church to victory and long-term sustainability. To God be the glory!

Top 10 Lies about Small Churches

10. Small churches are insignificant.
9. They can't impact their communities.
8. They have nothing to offer.
7. All small churches are inward focused.
6. All small churches are complacent.
5. All small churches are unhealthy.
4. All small churches have stale church services.
3. Small-church pastors have fewer skills.
2. God works more in large churches.
1. A church's smallness is a problem to fix, not an asset to maximize.*

Don't believe the lies! When small-church attendees believe such lies, their belief can result in a self-fulfilling prophecy. Your small congregation is just what many people in your community need, and it can do great things for God's kingdom!

---

*The beginning of each chapter has a list like the "Top 10" list above. I hope that anyone who wants to copy the lists and use them in their ministry will do so. Permission is granted to use the lists or other short quotes in your church or on your district or jurisdictional equivalent. Please retain my byline with any quoted material, including social media posts. Furthermore, quoted material that is included in another book or publication should abide by the usual documentation standards and, if length dictates, formal request standards.

ONE

Recognizing the Context

●————————————●

Therefore, I urge you, brothers and sisters, in view of God's mercy, to offer your bodies as a living sacrifice, holy and pleasing to God—this is your true and proper worship. Do not conform to the pattern of this world, but be transformed by the renewing of your mind. Then you will be able to test and approve what God's will is—his good, pleasing and perfect will.
—Rom. 12:1-2

Pastor Isaac was excited about the church growth at his small church. He had been the senior pastor for two years, and during that time, several new families had started attending. Two of the families even joined the church. Pastor Isaac was blessed with his church's moving forward after years of a plateau that previous pastors had not been able to navigate beyond. The church was doing better than it had done in over ten years, and district leadership was taking notice.

One Sunday morning when Pastor Isaac was feeling especially blessed, one of the new couples who had joined the church visited his office before Sunday school started. The couple had arrived at the church a year ago through the outreach efforts of a church lay leader. They had been attending another church but were searching for a different congregation because of a conflict at the previous church. They had been enthusiastic about their new church home and loved the authentic fellowship. Pastor Isaac had even counseled them through a particularly difficult time in their lives. In the process, they both spiritually grew and expressed an interest in volunteering in the church. They were doing so well that Pastor Isaac had even considered asking them if they would be interested in being mentored to teach a couple's Sunday school class. As they walked into his office this Sunday morning, he optimistically considered taking this opportunity to introduce the idea to them.

After the couple extended a warm greeting, they began to explain why they had arrived so early, and it wasn't so they could commit to a ministry mentorship. Quite the contrary, they were leaving the church! Pastor Isaac was stunned to silence as he listened to the couple explain that they had visited a larger church recently and loved the live band, professional praise team, and extensive ministry options so much that they just felt that church would be a better fit for them at this time in their lives.

Pastor Isaac did what any good pastor would do. He graciously embraced them, let them know he loved them, and wished them the best in their choice.

Once they left, he sat down in a puddle of discouragement and wondered why his small church's authentic environment had not been strong enough to make them want to stay. Little did he know that he would repeat a similar conversation two more times with two more couples before the year was up. By the end of his third year, the 20 percent increase in numerical growth his small church had achieved had declined to only 5 percent above the long-standing plateau level.

Nevertheless, a few new people had stayed with the church and put down spiritual roots. Furthermore, one long-attending family was a living example of God's intervention and redemption; the Lord had saved their marriage and provided new stability for their children. Despite these victories, Pastor Isaac allowed his focus on the people who left and the subsequent negative impact on numerical growth to cloud his vision of the spiritual and relational growth the church had experienced during his years as pastor there. Indeed, the church was showing some signs of progress, but Pastor Isaac's measure of success lay more with numerical growth than with spiritual or relational growth. The church's numerical average, even though it was somewhat higher than when he arrived, had not been sustained at the level he thought it should be.

Finally, he began to seriously doubt his abilities as a pastor in relation to leading this congregation. It didn't seem that he could engage many newcomers meaningfully enough to lead to their staying at the church long term. To further add to his dismay, several other prospective families visited once but never returned. When another family left, he even sensed that a board member suspected him of perhaps privately doing or saying something that was running off attendees. By the fourth year in his ministry, he began thinking that perhaps something was wrong with the church and that perhaps this assignment just wasn't a good one for him or the church. That's when Pastor Isaac accepted the call to another church in another state, with hopes that this new assignment would be a better church and a better fit.

What Pastor Isaac did not know was that pastors all over North America were experiencing the same phenomenon—people attending churches and shopping for churches based on the church's ability to better serve them. Furthermore, if he had tracked the families who left his small church for another church that offered more ministry options, he would have learned that most of those families had eventually left their new church for another that they believed offered them even better service. His church was just one stop on their church-shifting processional. Furthermore, he did not understand that the blame for the phenomenon did not rest with his ministry or the church, but with the impact of the consumer culture on the minds of attendees. According to Aaron B. James, "Consumer culture is not merely a threat to the church. It is the very field in which all churches (at least in Western locations) exist. Consumer culture . . . has colonized all of life. There is no location free from its influence for the church to plot its strategy."[1]

Meet Edward Bernays: The Father of the Consumer Culture

Arising during the early twentieth century, the modern consumer culture was greatly influenced by one man, Edward L. Bernays (1891–1995), a mastermind marketing guru.[2,3,4] Known as the King of Consumerism, the Great Manipulator, and a Father of Public Relations, Bernays was the nephew of Sigmund Freud. Bernays employed Gustave Le Bon's mass psychology, along with Freud's theories of the human subconscious yearnings, to create news-driven advertising to manipulate the masses to want more material possessions, not for need, but for greed, to gain value, merit, and notoriety.

Once mass producers understood the uncanny insight Bernays had into manipulating consumers, he became a sought-after commodity in the marketing world.[5,6,7] Bernays, who believed people were stupid, did indeed manipulate the twentieth-century consumer during his career that spanned eighty years.[8,9,10] Among many other ways he has influenced our culture, Bernays is the sole reason the taboo on women smoking cigarettes in public was demolished in the 1920s.[11] He is also the reason we eat bacon and eggs for breakfast.[12] Although he died in 1995, his manipulative influence is still alive and thriving, as manifested by the consumer mentality that colors many aspects of the global industrialized world.[13,14,15,16,17] Modern consumers in industrialized countries were born into a global climate where vendors have sought them out from childhood and have served them for their purchasing power.[18,19,20,21,22]

The Consumer Culture Meets the Church

However, the consumer mentality has not remained in the commercial world alone; it is now a strong influencer on the church environment of the United States.[23,24,25,26] In many cases, Christians are so blindly influenced by consumerism, it even drives the choice of where a person will attend church.[27,28,29,30] The consumer culture affects all churches, no matter the size. People have left one large church to attend another large church, not because the Lord led them, but because they liked the offerings of the other church better. Nevertheless, the consumer culture hits small churches harder than larger churches. Indeed, many small-church pastors and leaders feel defeated because they cannot compete in a consumer culture where, despite their best ministerial efforts, the bigger churches attract the most people.

Because of their consumer-culture conditioning, people often approach a church expecting the pastor and lay leaders to be in a Burger King mindset, ready to serve them a wide array of various ministries and programs. In the 1970s, Burger King had an advertisement with a jingle that went like this: "Hold the pickles. Hold the lettuce. Special orders don't upset us. All we ask is that you let us serve it your way. . . . Have it your way! Have it your way! Have it your way . . . at Burger King!" Burger King's most recent TV advertisement ends with the declaration, "You rule!" In other words, "Our fast-food chain will do whatever it takes so that you can have what you want and *exactly* what you want."

As already indicated, Burger King is not alone in this consumer-pleasing emphasis. The world is full of businesses that perpetually tell consumers they rule and that they should have the best service because of it. Unfortunately, since people are sent this message from birth, they don't even recognize that their minds have been shaped by the consumer force. Just as a fish born in murky water doesn't realize something is wrong with the water, so people born into consumerism don't realize that something about the way they are thinking about their church does not align with biblical truths. To be specific, the consumer culture affects the thinking of church attendees in many ways, including the following:

- Church shopping
- Expecting to be served
- Volunteering issues
- Sporadic attendance
- A lack of tithing
- Satisfied attendees with an inward focus

Church Shopping

People who visit one church after another for the primary purpose of determining what services a church has to offer that will best suit them are known as church shoppers. If Pastor Isaac had understood the characteristics of church shoppers, he would have been aware that the first couple who left a church to attend his church came to his church with a church-shopper mentality. When the initial excitement about their new small church wore off, their shopping list grew to a live band, a professional praise team, and more ministry services to please them. Church shoppers are consumer Christians who have allowed the consumer culture to drown out the voice of the Lord in directing them to a church. They usually don't care about correct or consistent theology any more than a diner at a restaurant cares if the menu offers Mexican, Asian, or American food; consumer Christians just want to be served.

It is important to note that a church shopper is not the same as a new family moving to town who visits several churches to earnestly discern where the Lord is leading them to attend. Visiting several churches is not a bad idea if a person is seriously seeking the Lord's will for where his or her family should attend church. However, such an exploration of determining God's will is not the same as visiting churches like a bargain hunter, looking for the best goods and services for the lowest investment.

Church shoppers want a church that has established programs and services that can best serve *them*. Unfortunately, church shoppers often mask their mission with the right words, such as "We're asking the Lord to lead us to the right church," which sounds spiritual, and they may even believe what they are saying. However, the "right church" will always be the place with the most programs that can *serve them* with the lowest investment *from them*. Furthermore, they may leave a church if there is even one change they don't like.

Expecting to Be Served

Once consumers decide to attend a church, they often arrive every week as if they are visiting a restaurant. They go in, sit down, and wait to be served, fully expecting the pastor and lay leaders to be singing the Burger King song, "Have it your way!" They look over the church bulletin as if looking at a restaurant menu and expect the best selections along with attentive service.

If they want a ministry that the church does not have listed, consumers are not usually shy about speaking up and suggesting that the pastor start such a ministry. However, since they expect to be served, they will no more offer to be involved in the ministry than they would consider helping a restaurant staff serve food. They are not usually interested in attending a church or staying at a church where they will be asked to invest time to help the church create the ministries they want. Many small-church pastors have watched a young couple drive away to never return because they wanted a full-blown children's program for their own children but were in no way interested in investing the time to get that program in place. They are there to be served, not to serve.

Volunteering Issues

When people expect to be served, rather than to serve, that leads to volunteering issues. They don't want to volunteer. However, if they do volunteer, they won't stay committed to the job they have agreed to do. Once the "feel good" vibe wears off, they may quit volunteering and go back to pew sitting and waiting to be served. The consumer culture blinds them to the reality that somebody is sacrificially serving so they can be served. They never consider that the question should not be, "What can my church do for me?" but "What can I do for my church?" They cannot see that a church will not thrive when the majority attend only to receive.

Ironically, people who refuse to volunteer will often adopt a critical attitude toward the pastor and lay leaders who seem to be "unaware" that the small church could "do so much better" if it offered a better children's program or a stronger youth meeting or live music during worship or a coffee bar. As already mentioned, consumer attendees often don't mind voicing their concerns. However, when they are asked to invest the time to, for instance, create a coffee bar and volunteer to serve in it, they may become exasperated, leave the church, and start church shopping all over again.

Sporadic Attendance

Consumers attend church just as they attend sporting events—when they want to—and they "sit in the bleachers," expecting church leaders (pastor and lay leaders) to faithfully be there and to always successfully perform like their sports team. They want all church posts filled so that they can have the best experience for the short time they will be in attendance. Sporadic attenders seem clueless of the fact that if every Christian decided to sporadically attend church, the church as we know it would cease to exist. They never think to themselves, *If I want my church to be there for me, I need to commit to weekly attendance and support, not just showing up once or twice a month or when I feel like it or when I don't have anything else to do.* The whole idea that the church needs their support and that the Lord wants to use them in the church is in no way part of their consumer thought process.

Contrary to this thought process, Christ calls us to deny ourselves, take up our cross, and follow him, to be crucified with him, to wholly live for him, no matter the cost (see Matt. 16:24; Gal. 2:20). Christ does not call us to embrace ourselves, sporadically cruise with him, and kind of live for him, expecting no cost.

A Lack of Tithing

If a person is attending church for what he or she will receive, then that person will not faithfully tithe. That person may donate a few dollars when he or she does choose to attend. After all, it would look bad to never donate to the church. However, a commitment to faithful tithing would mean that he or she would have to reduce his or her spending power, and that simply is not an option.

The consumer Christian may mask the lack of faithful giving with something like this: "My bills are just too much for me to be able to tithe; therefore, I will just give as I can." The truth is that many faithful tithers will testify that their bills seem to be too much for them to afford tithing. However, the Lord blesses the ones who tithe, and with his anointing, finances will usually align so that bills are met.

I recall a conversation I overheard nearly thirty years ago between two church lay leaders. Leader No. 1 was shopping for a new house, and he was expressing a strong temptation to stop paying his tithe so that he could afford a bigger house. Leader No. 2 said, "Now, we already talked about this, and you can't stop tithing just so you can have a bigger house." Ironically, there was nothing wrong with his house. It was larger than most, more beautiful than most. But he was determined to get a bigger, better house because that is the sort of stuff the consumer culture drives people to do. To the best of my knowledge, Leader No. 1, thankfully, didn't fall to the temptation. Nevertheless, the whole idea that he would be tempted in such a way is rooted in the consumer culture's pushing people to buy more, to own more, even if it means not tithing. At the same time, consumers will expect the pastor and lay leaders to have the funds to create the ministries they want, never considering that those ministries desperately need their tithes to operate. The result can be a church that is financially stuck, trying to create ministries with limited funding just as the Israelites were forced to make bricks without straw when they were under Egyptian oppression (Exod. 5).

Satisfied Attendees with an Inward Focus

Satisfied church attendees with an inward focus are happy with their church, just as a satisfied diner is happy with the restaurant service. They like everything just as it is. The church meets their perceived needs, and they think it's a great church. They have their friend group at church, and they love the fellowship. Be aware that there is nothing wrong with attendees being happy with their church, especially if they want to engage in outreach and invite other people. However, the satisfied attendee with an inward focus on "keeping the church the way I like it" prefers not to engage in community outreach, because having different people in attendance could change the church dynamics. Such a satisfied attendee may say, "Reaching out to people in this culture usually winds up creating a mess in the church. Outreach people have so many issues, which means trouble. The last thing our church needs is someone to come in and disrupt our church's harmony. Outreach is fine, but it needs to be to people who will fit in with us. I like our church just the way it is."

Such a mindset is also the product of the consumer culture because the satisfied attendee is a happy consumer. Happy consumers who always go to the same restaurant for the same meal fixed the same way will no longer be happy if the restaurant changes the recipe or the menu. Likewise, attendees with an inward focus have found a church that fits them and their needs, and nothing, not even Christ's Great Commission, can influence them to allow a change in the "church recipe or menu." These attendees have allowed the consumer culture to numb their minds to the point that they have forgotten that a major purpose of the church is to lead people to Christ, not to appease their own desires. This inward focus is as much a me-focus as the church shopper who cruises from one church to the next, browsing for the best ministries to meet his or her needs. The whole focus is on "making me happy."

The Consumer Culture's Impact on Small-Church Leadership

Since the consumer culture permeates the church world at large, it is inevitable that it also impacts small-church pastors and lay leaders. Unfortunately, there are a few people in ministry and church leadership who may fall prey to a ministry me-focus, ultimately expecting the church to serve them. However, more than likely, the pastor and core lay leaders are not me-focused. Rather, the consumer culture's impact on pastors and lay leaders can culminate in a negative force as they work hard to retain consumer attendees with as many ministries as possible. This impact also can take the form of both blatant and subconscious influence, including the following:

- Viewing the small church and pastor as insignificant
- The urge to "compete" with other churches
- Feeling overburdened
- Experiencing frustration and irritation
- Relational effects at home and church
- Spiritual effects
- Burnout
- Attrition
- Leaving the church to find a "better church"
- The foster-child syndrome

Viewing the Small Church and Pastor as Insignificant

Unfortunately, in a consumer culture that believes bigger is always better, small churches and their pastors are often viewed as less successful than large churches and their pastors, even though small churches collectively influence culture in mighty ways, as indicated in chapter 2. Unfortunately, small-church pastors and lay leaders can fall prey to believing this lie. It's important to remember that small-church pastors are not "small pastors" who don't work as hard as large-church pastors. Many small-church pastors are large in wisdom, insight, and people skills, all needed to maintain up-close, long-term relationships with parishioners. Furthermore, the committed small-church pastor is a great leader who will tirelessly work long hours to serve his or her congregation. While I believe it is time to re-define pastoral success, the church world still has ground to gain in this needed reform. True pastoral success should not be measured by the size of the church, but by the consecration of the pastor's heart and the obedience that flows from it. Unfortunately, small-church pastors and lay leaders can be convinced that their church and ministry are not as important as that of large churches, resulting in feelings of inferiority and insignificance.

The Urge to "Compete" with Other Churches

The consumer culture involves competition among businesses. The reason Burger King wants customers to know they can have their burger their way is because it can become a time-consuming issue to ask a fast-food restaurant to alter a food item. Thus, Burger King's competitive edge is that they *want* customers to customize their food choices.

Unfortunately, when a church's pastor and lay leaders start thinking in the same vein as Burger King by wondering "how our church can compete with other churches to attract the most people," they have fallen into consumer-culture quicksand. It's obvious that a small church cannot compete with a larger church in what it can offer consumer attendees any more than a small, family-owned store can compete with the massive selections of an international chain store. The small-church mantra "How can we even compete?" is a place of defeat with no answer. Nevertheless, no church should be thinking of competing against another church, no matter the size.

If the focus of church leadership is where it should be, the attention will be on sharing salvation, not coddling consumer Christians with all kinds of ministry bells and whistles just to get numbers higher. It's important to note that people who don't attend church and/or don't know Christ are not out church shopping. They aren't attending church, may have never attended church, and have no thought of looking for a church based on how it can serve them. When church leadership concentrates on reaching the lost and the unchurched, they will shift attention from competing with other churches to attract consumer Christians to doing what Christ has called us to do: "Go into all the world and preach the gospel" (Mark 16:15).

With that said, for decades, churches have used healthy competition among church attendees to inspire people to invite their friends and family to church. Years ago, we called them Sunday school campaigns or church attendance drives. The church people were divided into teams, and whichever team got the most people to attend was the winner. My husband recalls a competition like this from his childhood. His father, the Sunday school superintendent, and another lay leader were the team leaders for a Sunday school drive. The team leaders agreed that the leader who won the campaign would cut the loser's necktie in half and that the loser would have to wear a cutoff necktie throughout the entire church service. My husband's father's team won, so my husband's father got to cut off the other leader's necktie. This type of competition is fun and games for the purpose of a higher goal. It is also internal, within a church, among friends, and everybody is glad for anyone who visits the church, even if it's for the other team. This type of competition is harmless. It is not even close to the anguishing mindset that a small church's pastor and lay leaders can fall victim to when facing the stark realities of the consumer culture's impact on attendees and the futile urge to compete with other churches that evolves in the process.

Feeling Overburdened

While some consumer attendees are expecting to be served, devout leaders who are doing the serving can feel the brunt of the constant service demands that are placed on the backs of a few. I recall one tired lay leader saying, "If a ministry is going to be done, it will be from us." She pointed to the group of dedicated board members.

The urge to compete can contribute to the overburdened feelings of the faithful few. When church pastors and leaders start thinking they must compete with other churches, then they will start all kinds of new ministries that will hopefully attract more people. It's not unusual to see one layperson in a small church who serves in several positions. Sometimes, that one person is the pastor who drives the church van, teaches Sunday school, leads the worship service, and then preaches.

Experiencing Frustration and Irritation

When the few people who are doing most of the serving feel overburdened, frustration and irritation are often close behind. The frustration comes because those who are serving look around and see people who could serve but who are more interested in sitting in the pew and watching "the show." Next, the frustration breeds irritation at the people who could serve but are not serving. When irritation takes over, it affects relationships.

Relational Effects at Church and Home

Being in a state of frustration and irritation can place a person in a bad frame of mind, resulting in negative fallout on relationships in the church and at home. Unfortunately, frustration and irritation can spawn resentment. Resenting the consumer church attendees creates a bad vibe that attendees can sense, even if the resentment is never expressed. Some attendees may even decide to find another church because they interpret the resentment as "I'm not wanted at this church." Ironically, the very efforts that began as an attempt to be competitive and attract people can end up repelling people because of the frustration, irritation, and resentment that result from a few people "jumping through hoops" to make the church attractive for consumers.

Furthermore, when a person is frustrated and irritated at church, then there will be less patience for the issues awaiting that person at home. Being snappish is just the beginning of the behavior an exhausted pastor or church servant may manifest in the home. Relationships at home can thus become tense and strained. Any children still at home or the spouse—who may be one of the exhausted servants—can then join in the misery.

Spiritual Effects

When the faithful few are overburdened because they are overserving, they can have less time for investing in their own spiritual welfare and growth. When a pastor or layperson is "running off in all directions," spending personal time with the Lord may become an afterthought. However, as chapter 3 indicates, that time with God should be the well from which Christian service springs forth, not "one more thing to do on a checklist that makes me tired just looking at it."

Furthermore, while frustration and irritation are emotions that we can choose to effectively deal with, resentment is a cancer of the soul, eating away joy, peace, and contentment. The spiritual effects may be catastrophic, which is why it is so important to place a premium on staying rooted in the Word of God and letting nothing replace the devotion to being still and knowing that he is God (Ps. 46:10). No matter how much time is allocated to trying to attract and keep consumer Christians, no pastor or lay leader, no matter how great he or she is, can continually appease the consumer because the consumer mindset simply won't stop without divine intervention.

Burnout

As we will discuss in chapter 7, burnout is a trap that pastors and lay leaders may fall into, with special emphasis on the pastor. Often, the word "burnout" is thrown around loosely as an indicator of physical exhaustion. However, true burnout happens when a person is physically, spiritually, mentally, and emotionally exhausted. Unfortunately, I have heard people speak of pastors who are burned out in a negative way, as if the pastor somehow chose burnout. One critical person even stated that all pastors who experienced burnout did so because they had emotional problems to start with. However, burnout can creep in on even an emotionally healthy person, bit by bit, unrecognized until it has taken over. While many people have written on burnout and its causes, my recent study discovered a link between burnout and a lack of education about the consumer culture.[31] When consumer attendees are determined to arrive at church to receive, the few that are doing all the giving can eventually give out, resulting in burnout.

Attrition

Unfortunately, when burnout happens, attrition can also happen. Some laypeople who have carried the load of service can get so exhausted that they "take a break from church for a season" and then never return, or if they do return, they come back as observers, not participants. Some pastors can walk away from the ministry altogether. A lack of understanding of the consumer culture and how it affects the ones who are overserving can lead to the misconception that the ones serving must be doing something wrong and are, thus, repelling attendees. Therefore, if burnout hasn't fully occurred, a pastor or lay leader may leave the church for another church.

Leaving the Church to Find a "Better Church"

If we aren't careful, both pastors and lay leaders can fall into the trap of searching for a church in a consumer mindset and changing churches outside of God's will. Like Pastor Isaac, who did not understand that the consumer culture was causing the challenges in church growth, church lay leaders, and especially pastors, can start doubting their abilities in their current settings. They may even become convinced that something is wrong with their current church. The result of either thought process is that a pastor may try to find a "better church" that will "better fit" his or her ministry or needs, not realizing that the next church will struggle with the same consumer issues all churches in North America experience.

Granted, there are some church assignments that might not be a good fit for the pastor or congregation, for whatever reason. When such a mismatch happens, it's good for the pastor to recognize the misfit and find another congregation where he or she can thrive in ministry. However, the point is that when the consumer culture is driving the issues, then the consumer culture is to be blamed, not the pastor or lay leaders, and the church should be navigated in a way that negates the consumer culture.

The Foster-Child Syndrome

When children are removed from their own family environment and placed with a foster family, the effects can be traumatic, especially if a child is beyond infancy. The trauma can be increased when a child is moved from one foster home to another. The child may choose not to bond with the foster parents because he or she fears that the parents, who may *seem* to be extending love, will eventually reject him or her anyway. Foster children, and even adopted children, may be plagued with fears of abandonment to the point that they will have nightmares about their parents throwing them away in the garbage or in a dumpster. These types of nightmares only entrench the children's decision not to bond with the foster parents because the children are convinced, based on their life experiences, that rejection is inevitable. Therefore, when the rejection happens, it will hurt less if the child's heart is not fully involved. Furthermore, some foster children and adoptees will even act out in defiant and mean ways in an attempt to repel the foster or adoptive parents and speed up the inevitable rejection. Their thought process goes something like this: *Since they are going to reject me anyway, I might as well speed up the process and get it over with.* I refer to these issues as the foster-child syndrome.

The foster-child syndrome may also manifest in the hearts and minds of small-church laypeople and pastors. Laypeople are affected by the foster-child syndrome when they have watched one pastor after another come into the church, only to leave in a few years. The pastor may arrive with big plans to do great things in the church, but, like Pastor Isaac, his or her enthusiasm soon fizzles, resulting in a resignation. After years of a pastoral revolving door, the long-standing core of devout small-church laypeople will share a family bond with each other, but they won't bond with the new pastor. Like foster children who are convinced they will once again experience rejection, such lay-people may be thinking multiple things, such as the following:

- *This new pastoral family seems great, but they will probably not be with us long.*
- *If our small church does start growing, this pastor will become a hot commodity and will then move to another bigger church.*
- *Our small church is just a career stepping-stone for this pastor. He/She doesn't really love us.*
- *Since the pastor is going to leave soon, anyway, what's the use in sharing in his/her vision for ministry?*
- *We might as well go ahead and run off this pastor by being uncooperative and argumentative and get the rejection over with.*

Meanwhile, pastors who have seen consumer attendees come into their small church only to leave for a "bigger, better church" may also experience the foster-child syndrome. In this frame of mind, the pastor may keep a relational distance from attendees because he or she has been rejected so many times, he or she is afraid of getting too close, especially to newcomers who may have arrived from another church. After years of seeing consumer attendees come and go, a pastor may start thinking, *It's best not to connect with this family because they'll probably be leaving soon anyway.* The newcomers may sense the disconnect, which leads them to search for another church where they can connect.

When the foster-child syndrome impacts both small-church laypeople and the pastor, they can be caught in a negative cycle of behavior that feeds on itself. The result is the inevitable rejection, the fear of which is driving the foster-child thought process in the first place. Thus, the foster-child syndrome itself stimulates a self-fulfilling prophecy, and just as some foster children create a scenario that leads to the rejection they are afraid of, so small-church laypeople and pastors may do the same. And the whole thing is a product of the consumer culture.

Navigating the Consumer Culture

The Balance

After reading this chapter, it would be very easy to go into consumer-culture reject mode and stop all shopping, never eat at a fast-food restaurant again, cease giving Christmas and birthday presents, avoid spending a dime unless it's absolutely necessary, and rail against the ills of our consumer culture. However, the purpose of this book, among other things, is to make readers aware that the consumer culture does exist, to inform them of the impact it can have on churches, and to provide solutions that will help pastors and lay leaders navigate their churches to growth, despite the consumer culture.

The purpose of this book is not to stimulate a consumer-culture reject mode, to demonize people who make a living as a product of the consumer culture, or to say all marketing professionals, advertisers, or public relations people are cold-hearted manipulators. Many good people who love the Lord and are fully committed to him and give their tithes and sacrificial offerings are also business owners, including fast-food restaurateurs, who operate in a consumer culture and who use marketing concepts to advertise their businesses. A devout Christian car dealership owner may pray for customers to come buy new cars as he or she looks out on a car lot crowded with new vehicles. A Christian clothing store owner may pray that the Lord will send a wave of customers, eager to buy, so that he can make a profit this quarter. A devoted Christian online reseller may praise the Lord that she has just paid $5.00 for an item she can make a quick $200 profit on. None of these endeavors or prayers are evil.

Even in the Bible, there are examples of merchants selling their goods. For instance, in the New Testament, we see Lydia, a seller of purple (Acts 16:14-15), and Paul was a tentmaker (18:3). Even though the consumer culture had not reached the forceful impact of today's world, it's probable that New Testament businesspeople were still praying for customers to buy their goods just as merchants do today. When customers bought from New Testament merchants, I'm sure the devout merchant considered it an answer to prayer. Likewise, today, it can be an act of obedience to the Lord when he prompts us to purchase items that we may not necessarily need from such merchants when that merchant desperately needs our business. While helping people can come in the form of giving to meet a need, it can also come in the form of buying what a hardworking person is selling.

The point is that, as Christians, we must be truly Spirit led, not consumer driven, and we must surrender both our giving and our spending to him. Furthermore, we should fully allow the Lord, not the consumer culture, to drive our decision of the church we will pastor or attend and that once we have arrived at that church, we will be there to invest our time and efforts to bring about the furtherance of the gospel, not the appeasement of our own consumer demands. Romans 12:1-2 states, "Therefore, I urge you, brothers and sisters, in view of God's mercy, to offer your bodies as a living sacrifice, holy and pleasing to God—this is your true and proper worship. *Do not conform to the pattern of this world*, but be transformed by the renewing of your mind. Then you will be able to test and approve what God's will is—his good, pleasing and perfect will" (emphasis added). The consumer culture is a pattern of this world, and we who are wholly consecrated to Christ should resist allowing the consumer mindset to conform us so that we are obeying consumer impulses, rather than obeying the Lord. We are to be in the world but not of the world (John 17:13-19).

The Commitment

Thankfully, God is bigger and more powerful than the consumer culture. He doesn't shop for churches. He anoints consecrated worshippers, no matter the church size. Under his anointing, God grows his kingdom in ways that are seen and unseen.

Nevertheless, some small churches are teetering on the precipice of closure within the next few years. These churches often can be revived and renewed. However, they need long-term pastors who will overcome obstacles and diligently labor to navigate them to health. They need committed laypeople who will work side by side with pastors to invest the time and effort needed for future sustainability. Many small churches require pastors with the heart of a "tentmaker" missionary—pastors who will resist caving to the consumer culture, who will commit long term to a church family, and who will work another job, if necessary (see chap. 7). Such pastors will not consider using a small church as a stepping-stone to further their ministry careers but will focus on the sustainable future of their churches and let God take care of their ministry careers. Granted, there are times when the Lord does call a small-church pastor to another small church or even to a larger church. Large churches need pastors too. However, this change means having a full understanding that moving from one church to the next, regardless of size, is because of the Lord's leading, not the consumer culture's bidding. With these truths in mind, the time has come to give credence to small-church pastors and lay leaders who remain committed to their calling and their small church, even in a consumer culture.

The Plan

Instead of allowing the consumer culture to influence leaving a church or leaving ministry altogether, it's better to develop a realistic plan for growing the small church in a consumer culture, and this book will continue to guide you to do exactly that. Along with consistently teaching the doctrine of entire sanctification, which includes a full consecration to Christ (see chap. 3), part of that plan should include the effective education of all church attendees about the consumer culture and how it can affect people. The only way consumer Christians can find freedom is through teaching that gently and lovingly makes them aware of the problem and guides them to a full consecration to Christ.

There is no way around the consumer culture's influence, but people who have not been made aware of the impact of the consumer culture on their minds will very likely go into denial, claiming they have not been influenced or impacted by consumerism. As already mentioned, they are like fish born in murky water who can't see the debris in the water because they have never known anything else. The fish are conditioned from birth to function in the unclear water and have no clue there is clear water available, so they think they are doing just fine. Likewise, people who are blinded to the consumer culture's impact may truly believe they are changing churches through

God's leading when it's really all about what they want in a church as a consumer.

None of this is to say that every person who attends a church is engaging with the church as a consumer. However, all of us have been impacted by the consumer culture in some way. For instance, devout small-church lay leaders and pastors may have exhausted themselves to attract and keep consumers at their church with few to no results. In such a situation, education about the consumer culture is freeing because it answers the *why* question about the struggle to retain attendees. If you find yourself in such a situation, be encouraged! This book offers concepts that will help you lead your church to health, despite the consumer culture.

If God has called you, he will go before you, he will surround you with his mercy, he will provide for the journey, and he won't stop, even when you want to.

PAUSING TO PLAN

At the end of each chapter, there are questions that should be discussed among the pastor and lay leaders. Ideally, the pastor and lay leaders will read one chapter at a time and meet after each chapter for a discussion and planning session. One of the keys for success in the sessions is for pastors and lay leaders alike to honestly share their thoughts, which can happen in a nonjudgmental environment. The "Pausing to Plan" segment after each chapter establishes a framework for the pastor and lay leaders to collaborate (see chap. 5 for more on collaborative leadership) to create a plan for their church as they move into the future.

The questions in chapter 1 are intended to inspire readers to recognize how the consumer culture may be impacting you, your thought process, and your church so that, as you plan, you will understand the context and obstacles the consumer culture presents. Recognizing specific ways the consumer culture has impacted your church also helps to relieve frustration because you realize that the consumer-driven issues and struggles are not the fault of the church, the pastor, or lay leaders, but the fault of the cultural impact on the minds of attendees.

As you move into pondering the questions below, it is tempting to shy away from admitting that the consumer culture may have impacted you personally. However, such an admission doesn't mean that you are currently approaching your church in a consumer mindset. Small churches would not exist if every pastor and lay leader were in the church with a me-focused consumer mindset. However, admitting the effects of the consumer culture simply recognizes that the consumer culture we live in does affect each of us in some way. For instance, someone might admit that he or she recently made an impulse purchase.

Furthermore, consider that the consumer-culture effect may even be against our own choices. For instance, a smaller, family-owned business shuts down because a competing national chain comes into town, and the community consumers flock to the new business, disregarding the years of faithful service the family-owned business has provided, thus causing a church leader or spouse to lose employment.

As you pause to ponder the questions below, think hard, dig deep, and thoroughly discuss each prompt:

- Each participant should choose at least one key concept he or she found especially meaningful or applicable to your church. As a group, discuss all the key concepts each participant has chosen.
- How has the consumer culture impacted me personally?
- How has the consumer culture impacted the way people view our small church, including members/attendees, visitors, the church world at large?
- How has the consumer culture tangibly impacted our church in ways that can be counted or documented?
- How can we educate church attendees about the consumer culture's impact in ways that they will receive it and make changes in their hearts and thought processes as needed?

Top 10 Advantages of Small Churches

10. You can't get lost in a small church.

9. The bathrooms are easy to find.

8. When your toddler runs to the platform during the sermon, it's viewed as holy entertainment.

7. Christmas programs are full of bloopers, and that's what makes them so great.

6. If you have to stop and restart your special song, nobody cares.

5. It's OK to interrupt the song service with a testimony, and the more the better.

4. Your kids have multiple sets of parents and grandparents.

3. Your prayer requests are in the church bulletin.

2. If you miss church without reporting in, there is a churchwide alert to find you.

1. You have a close relationship with your pastor.

The family bond that happens in small churches is vital to the kingdom of God. The time has come to recognize small churches as the powerful spiritual network that they are.

TWO

Realizing the Advantages

●────────────●

Finally, brothers and sisters, whatever is true, whatever is noble, whatever is right, whatever is pure, whatever is lovely, whatever is admirable—if anything is excellent or praiseworthy—think about such things.
—Phil. 4:8

In July 2019, I wrote "The Top 10 Advantages of Small Churches" in a five-minute whirlwind that I now have identified as a holy download from the Lord. I never planned the list; it just came to my mind and exited through my fingers. Within about twenty minutes of writing the list, I had created a Facebook image that I posted to my Wesleyan Woman Facebook page. To my utter astonishment, the post immediately went viral with no boosting, culminating in three spontaneous viral episodes with a reach of over three million people, including hundreds of thousands of shares, likes, and comments across denominational lines, from the Nazarenes to the Baptists to the Pentecostals to the Presbyterians to the Episcopalians. I was completing my doctoral dissertation that focused on the educational deficits of small-church pastors, and I was still in a mindset of developing concepts to get small churches to grow into larger congregations.

Consequently, when the Top 10 list immediately went viral, I never expected it. Quite the contrary, I had a few negative thoughts as I was posting the list. I speculated that the post would not receive much attention because it contained so many words. With social media posts, the shorter they are, the more likely they are to gain attention. Thankfully, the Lord does not act according to our negative thoughts or social media trends. He is the one from whom the post originated, and he took over its distribution. I believe it went viral through the power of the Holy Spirit just as it was inspired through the power of the Holy Spirit. The Lord used the experience to teach me some important truths. While the Top 10 list bounced from north to south, east to west, all over North America like a whirling cyber tennis ball, it turned into a spiritual and mental hurricane that changed my perspective within a few days.

As I read all the enthusiastic comments from small-church attendees who were declaring the benefits of their small churches and using the Top 10 list to invite people to visit their churches, I swiftly realized that throngs of people across denominational lines all over the United States and Canada *love* small churches (a few people to one hundred in attendance). I experienced a new level of joy over the fact that small churches cover North America and many parts of the world. Furthermore, the Lord immediately showed me that despite the consumer culture and all the difficulties it presents, small churches are the backbone of the church world, and it's a grave error when people view small churches as insignificant and lacking influence.

Another realization that hit me was that I, too, love small churches. After all, I am the product of the small church. I have attended small churches most of my life, and so has my husband.

Our family roots go back to the same small Nazarene church in East Texas where I now copastor with my husband. My extended family has historically attended small churches. My father pastored small churches. Some of my favorite memories happened in small churches with some of my favorite people. At the time of my posting the Top 10 list, my husband and I had even copastored another small church for over eleven years.

Almost overnight, God did a work in my heart through that viral post and rekindled and solidified my love for small churches and the pastors and people who worship there. That's when I realized how wrong I had been to try to create concepts that would instruct small churches to become something they are not. Assuming that small churches should grow to large churches for them to be successful is foundational to assuming that spiritual impact rests in church size and that all people would rather attend a large church. Those assumptions simply aren't true. Spiritual impact rests in the power of the gospel of Jesus Christ and the Holy Spirit at work in the lives of believers. Furthermore, throngs of people prefer to attend a small church. This is not a spiritual issue; it's a personal preference. The reality is that if all small churches grow into big churches, throngs of people will not have their optimum ministry point.

Three Truths about Small Churches

In a world where bigger means better, it is easy to adopt a consumer mindset when we consider small churches. Too many times, small churches are viewed as less successful and less important than large churches, simply because they are small. However, there are great advantages to small churches, and there are unchurched people in every community who would enjoy those advantages. As they testified with the Top

10 list, there are people all over the United States and Canada who *do* enjoy those advantages.

Given the reality of the small-church impact, three truths about small churches should be considered:

- God has moved and will move through small churches.
- There is a powerful connection that can happen in small churches that can transform people's lives one at a time.
- If Satan can discourage small-church pastors and leaders, they will be blinded to the advantages of small churches and the amazing ways God can use them and is using them.

God Moves through Small Churches

God has historically moved and will continue to move through small churches. To be successful in the small-church setting, the leadership team must shift focus from the consumer culture's influence that points to all the ways the small church can't measure up to a large church to how it *can* function in small-church victory through the power of the Lord moving upon it! When we look at small churches in a consumer mindset, we can forget that the early church was made up of small house churches. So many times, we can focus on the thousands of people present on the day of Pentecost and think that such a gathering should be the norm and that if it isn't the norm, something is spiritually wrong with the church. The problem is that the day of Pentecost wasn't replicated on a weekly basis in the New Testament, nor is it necessary for the day of Pentecost to be replicated today as a criterion that the Holy Spirit is moving in a church. Just as a multitude of people today worship in small churches, so New Testament believers regularly worshipped in small house churches. Each of these churches usually consisted of a nucleus of fifteen to twenty people.[1]

In recent history, Yoido Full Gospel Church, a South Korean church that is considered the largest church in the world, was eventually organized as a collection of small groups, or house churches, mainly led by women. Each small nucleus of believers that meets in a house during the week joins with other nuclei for one of several massive Sunday worship services. But the day-to-day connection and care for the congregation happens in small, home-based family groups. The pastor who set up this model, Cho Yong-gi, also known as David Cho, claimed that when he had exhausted his abilities as a pastor to keep up the demands of a large congregation, he established the house-church model.[2]

Any savvy large-church pastor knows that his or her congregation will function best if it is organized into small groups, like several small churches, where people can form bonds with fellow members. Therefore, the healthiest large churches will replicate what happens in small churches and be modeled after the Korean church on some level, with the small groups meeting within the church or in people's homes. The main point is that God has used and continues to use small cell groups of believers to carry out the work of his kingdom. Small churches should rejoice in knowing that they have an opportunity to partner with the Lord to do what he has done and continues to do through small family groups that commit their efforts to him.

A Powerful Connection in Small Churches

There is a powerful family connection that can happen in small churches that can transform people's lives one at a time. Many small churches don't have extensive programs, a big praise team, or high-tech buildings, but they do have the most important things: God's anointing, family connections, and prayer support that won't stop!

This strong family connection is what can draw people back to a small church. As already mentioned, despite the consumer culture, a multitude of people in the United States and Canada prefer to attend a small church, and it's a preference the Lord understands, as indicated in his establishing small house churches in the New Testament. I believe the strong family connection is an element that makes people love small churches so much.

Unfortunately, when we focus on changing small churches into what they are not, we miss the mighty work of God in what they are. There is nothing bigger than God's love and nothing much better than experiencing that love with his family, and that includes in a small church.

Satan's Discouragement

A small-church team may become discouraged because they cannot offer the latest trend. But there is no trend that can compete with the classic love, fellowship, and family support that their church can offer. However, if Satan can discourage small-church pastors and lay leaders, they will be blinded to the advantages of small churches and the amazing ways God can use them and is using them.

Like the thief in Jesus's parable about the good shepherd, Satan wants to "steal and kill and destroy" (John 10:10). He wants to steal the vision from small-church leadership, kill their desire to reach out to their communities, and destroy any scrap of optimism they might have about their congregation. Understand that Satan will use whatever means he can to achieve this goal, whether that be the consumer culture or other forces. However, small-church pastors and lay leaders don't have to succumb to Satan's discouraging blows.

Asset Thinking

Spirit-led asset thinking is a deep well of holy positivity that can contribute to overriding Satan's defeat and can mobilize small-church believers to do the will of the Father. Asset thinking is the opposite of deficit thinking, which is a focus on all the things the small church does not have and cannot do because of its limited resources. Philippians 4:8 is the theme verse for the small-church asset thinker: "Finally, brothers and sisters, whatever is true, whatever is noble, whatever is right, whatever is pure, whatever is lovely, whatever is admirable—if anything is excellent or praiseworthy—think about such things." When leaders focus on their small church's assets, rather than its deficits, they will value the good the church can offer and want to share that good with others. When a small church's pastor and lay leaders praise church members about the advantages of small churches and what their church does right, it results in a morale shift from defeat and discouragement to victory for both pastor and people! Small-church believers can thus celebrate their strengths and build on them rather than allowing "what they are not" to make them feel inadequate.

One Indiana small-church pastor saw her congregation attendance double from twenty-plus to forty-plus because she changed one thing: her perspective on the value of her small church.[3] This small-church pastor tapped into a powerful reality about asset thinking: a change in perspective means a change in direction, and a change in direction means new life. Focusing on the advantages of all small churches, as well as the advantages specific to your small church, is part of the stuff that asset thinking is made of.

Advantages of Small Churches: Collective

Statistics indicate that small churches are part of something *huge* that God is doing all over the world. Well-known small-church author Karl Vaters indicates that of the 2.2 billion Christians in the world, including Catholics and Protestants, over half of them choose to worship in smaller congregations.[4] That's over 1 billion people! In 2022, and many years before, the small-church category for my denomination (99 and fewer) collectively had higher attendance, more new members, and higher missions giving than any other church-size category.[5] The 2022 chart (fig. 2.1) represents the latest statistics available at the writing of this book. These statistics are reflective of post-COVID numbers, and in the United States and Canada the number of small churches in the "99 and fewer" category is at 82 percent. The global figures for the denomination, which are also included in figure 2.1, feature an even higher percentage of churches that have 99 and fewer in attendance, which is 89 percent.

However, before COVID, the "99 and fewer" category was not excessively lower. For Sunday morning worship, nearly half of the denomination's churches (49 percent) averaged 50 or fewer people in attendance, and 75 percent of the churches averaged 99 or fewer people.[6] The denomination is in alignment with the North American church attendance dynamics. In the United States during the years before COVID, 70 percent of Protestant churches averaged 100 or fewer in attendance, and 44 percent of Protestant churches averaged 50 or fewer in attendance.[7]

With that said, the 2022 statistics for the Church of the Nazarene in figure 2.1 show the great work small churches collectively achieved in attendance, new members, and giving. Again, if you are serving the Lord in another denomination, I encourage you to consult the statistics from your denomination. It is astonishing to consider that the small church is collectively the backbone of the church world across denominational lines; each small church should be valued as such. As you examine the chart, add the highlighted categories together ("Less than 50" and "50 to 99") and compare the small-church totals with the totals from the remaining individual categories ("100 to 249," "250 to 499," "500 to 999," and "1,000 or More").

Congregation Sizes for the USA/Canada Region, Church of the Nazarene: 2022

Worship Size Category	# of Churches	# of Worshippers	# of New Nazarenes	WEF Giving	% of Churches	% of Worshippers	% of New Nazarenes	% of WEF Giving
Less than 50	2,980	66,884	4,236	$ 6,859,618	60%	18%	22%	19%
50 to 99	1,116	76,917	4,711	$ 8,059,035	22%	21%	25%	22%
100 to 249	632	94,894	4,934	$ 9,969,356	13%	26%	26%	27%
250-499	162	53,771	2,004	$ 5,430,255	3%	15%	10%	15%
500 to 999	59	39,587	2,338	$ 3,701,678	1%	11%	12%	10%
1,000 or More	20	29,838	887	$ 2,612,615	0%	8%	5%	7%
Totals	4,969	361,891	19,110	$36,632,557	100%	100%	100%	100%

Note: Includes all active churches and NewStarts

Congregation Sizes for the Global Church of the Nazarene: 2022

Worship Size Category	# of Churches	# of Worshippers	# of New Nazarenes	WEF Giving	% of Churches	% of Worshippers	% of New Nazarenes	% of WEF Giving
Less than 50	20,016	331,457	37,042	$ 7,293,274	69%	24%	33%	19%
50 to 99	5,728	402,840	36,322	$ 8,403,225	20%	29%	32%	22%
100 to 249	2,562	360,483	26,134	$10,658,341	9%	26%	23%	28%
250 to 499	427	137,471	6,443	$ 5,545,482	1%	10%	6%	14%
500 to 999	105	71,207	4,538	$ 3,724,796	0%	5%	4%	10%
1,000 or More	41	90,843	2,685	$ 2,622,513	0%	7%	2%	7%
Totals	28,879	1,394,301	113,164	$38,247,631	100%	100%	100%	100%

Note: Includes all active churches and NewStarts

Fig. 2.1. Congregation sizes for the Church of the Nazarene: 2022

The total number of new members in the highlighted categories for the United States and Canada is 8,947; when divided by the number of days in a year, the total is about 25 people per day. This encouraging number reminds me of the Scripture that states, "And the Lord added to their number daily" (Acts 2:47). Indeed, the Lord is adding daily to the numbers of the church, and he is using small churches to generate the biggest increase per day, per year.

These revealing statistics reflect the reality of other denominations around the world. They remind us that we must avoid measuring a church's success by its size. When we do so, we remain blinded to God's amazing work in even the smallest of congregations. For instance, in the Church of the Nazarene, all churches declined in attendance during the COVID pandemic except the churches in the "0 to 25" category, and this size church saw an 8.25 percent increase in attendance during the pandemic.[8] This statistic is an important reminder that, regardless of the denomination, the kingdom of God is not about the size of the building, but the size of Christ's love in the people's hearts. Small churches are so important to God that he personally meets his followers there, just as he does in large churches. Whether the church is large or small, he woos others to him through those churches. According to Vaters,

> If Small Churches are a problem to be fixed, . . . do we really believe that over one billion of our fellow believers are mistaken because of the size of the church in which they've chosen to worship and serve God? They're not mistaken at all. It's time to stop treating Small Churches, the pastors who lead them and the people who worship God in them as inadequate, as failures, as problems to be fixed or as obstacles to be overcome. . . . Small Churches are not small

because of human weakness, lack of planning or short-term vision. Small Churches are not a problem. They are an essential element in a divine strategy.[9]

As a small-church pastor or lay leader, it's important to remember that, collectively, small churches are like single grains of salt scattered across the land. Together, they spiritually season the whole nation. One of the qualities of salt is that it disappears into the food, and so many times small-church pastors and lay leaders can feel as if their churches are so small that they are almost invisible to the eyes of the world. However, Jesus said, "You are the salt of the earth" (Matt. 5:13*a*), and we can take heart in knowing that, according to statistics, small churches are *very salty!* Thus, they are not invisible to God. Every small-church pastor and lay leader needs to weekly remind themselves that what may seem like an insignificant church gathering is part of a mass of people that God is empowering to further his kingdom. Small-church leaders must view the impact of small churches collectively and remind themselves that they are part of something really big, even if the individual church average may seem small.

Advantages of Small Churches: Individual

As the statistics indicate, small churches have collective advantages. However, they also have individual advantages. The "Top 10 Advantages of Small Churches" list, found at the first of this chapter, reflects some foundational advantages that most small churches manifest:

- The whole church is in a family relationship.
- Children of all ages attend the Sunday morning worship service.
- They often have a more relaxed atmosphere.

- They offer up-front opportunities for those still learning.
- You *won't* get lost in a small church.

The Whole Church Is in a Family Relationship

All successful churches, no matter the size, will be relational. The relationships in any size church can be as close as that of a biological family. However, the small church is highly relational because everyone knows everyone, and that includes the pastoral family. The small-group aspect of a small church leads to most, if not all, attendees belonging to a tight-knit family group where they can connect across generational lines as brothers and sisters in Christ. Thus, if you have children, they will gain multiple sets of parents and grandparents as fellow church members become like family.

Not only can strong relational connections happen among attendees, but also there can be an opportunity for the pastor to develop a closer relationship with attendees. Small-church pastors see their congregants up close on a regular basis. They learn to work together, to pray together, and to relate together, especially if a pastor remains at a church long term. While it's not advisable for a pastor to act toward congregants as their therapist, there still can be and should be the development of an anointed friendship that places the pastor in a position where he or she can be a strong influence in the lives of attendees, including children and teens. Many pastors feel the call of God for ministry in a small church, and some of them testify to having had the same small-church pastor involved in their lives from childhood. The impact of a pastor who is willing to commit long term to a congregation and stay close may not be recognized until eternity, but it is vitally important. A small church offers a highly relational context for these types of connections.

Children Included in Sunday Morning Worship

The Top 10 list states that "when your toddler runs to the platform during the sermon, it's viewed as holy entertainment." That's because the presence of children in the main church service is cherished and embraced in the small-church setting. Hence, they are included in Sunday morning services in many small churches, especially the churches that average fewer than fifty.

One of my favorite memories from pastoring in a small church is the time I was preaching about the importance of being thankful for the "here and now" time the Lord has given each of us. I was saying that too many times, parents say they'll be glad when their children can walk. Then they'll be glad when their children are in school. Next, parents say they'll be glad when their children are in junior high . . . then high school, so they can drive, . . . then college. And the next thing you know, such parents have wished away their children's entire lives and missed fully enjoying those precious few days the children were at home because they, the parents, were so busy seeing the negatives in the present and wishing for the future to be better.

Anyway, God has an amazingly wonderful sense of humor. Literally, as I was saying those very words, a toddler broke loose from the back pew. The child's mom is a nurse, and she had to be on duty that Sunday morning. So the father had faithfully come alone to church and brought his two little girls with him. The cotton-haired toddler, who loved my husband and me and loved sitting on the platform with us, was not going to be confined to the back pew any longer and wanted to get in on the platform action. Like a bouncing bunny rabbit, she whizzed up a side aisle, making a straight line to the platform, with the father trotting close behind her. The father, a Harley-Davidson motorcycle enthusiast, was dressed in black leather and jeans, with the chains and tattoos to go with it. As he reached to snatch his daughter, the chains clanked a bit, as if they were laughing at his near miss. The toddler wasn't deterred; she kept running forward until she made it to the platform.

And there I was, standing behind the pulpit, preaching my heart out. As the toddler dashed behind me, and her chain-clanking father followed close after, I was saying, "We need to treasure our precious children at each stage of their lives and be thankful that the Lord has blessed us with such a wonderful gift."

The toddler, now enjoying the chase, exited the platform and darted up the left side of the sanctuary. The father finally caught up with her about halfway to the back of the sanctuary, scooped her up, and plunked her down on the back pew where the whole escapade started.

The memory is priceless. By the grace of God, I was able to stay focused and never missed a beat in my sermon. The congregation, although somewhat distracted, even remained attentive to my words—well, sorta! Nevertheless, I wouldn't trade the memory for any worship service where everything went smoothly. I will never forget it, and neither will the approximately thirty attendees who saw the whole thing. Once that memorable worship service was over, we all had a good laugh and included the father in it. He had no need to feel embarrassed or bad. We were all too blessed by the rare, zany moment to be offended. It was, indeed, holy entertainment.

With all due respect, you usually don't get that kind of holy entertainment in a church that averages five thousand in attendance, because the toddlers are all in the nursery. Don't get me wrong. I'm not opposed to nursery-equipped churches with thousands in attendance. More power to them as they reach the culture for Christ! But there is something special about a small church with such a supportive family atmosphere that everyone is thrilled to see the babies and children in full force during the main church service, whatever that might entail. According to Helopoulos,

> Children learn from their parents and the rest of the congregation. But they also set an example for the covenant community. When Jesus blesses the children, he says: "[Let the children come to me; do not hinder them,] for to such belongs the kingdom of God. Truly, I say to you, whoever does not receive the kingdom of God like a child shall not enter it" (Mark 10:14-15 [ESV]). Many consider children a distraction in corporate worship, but in Christ's eyes, they're an example.[10]

Many small churches don't have the volunteer base to support children's church, or even a nursery, every Sunday. So the nursery might be offered as needed, and children's church, if it is in function, may be offered only once or twice a month. As much as we may want to think a lack of weekly children's church is a bad thing, it's actually a good thing for children to regularly attend the adult worship service. When children spend their whole lives sequestered away, apart from the adult worship experience, they lose connection with the realities of the church world. Beth Bidle-Rush, a long-time children's pastor and retreat director for Equip to Engage: Leadership Development for Children's Ministry, fully supports the inclusion of children in corporate worship. Bidle-Rush states, "We've missed something when we've disconnected children from the whole body. They become like a detached arm."[11] When they aren't in the worship service, they don't witness the impromptu testimonies that can be common in a small church. They aren't present when the church body gathers to pray or when a seeker responds at the end of the service. They don't get to hear the pastor's sermons, which they can understand way more than we may realize. Instead, for their whole childhood, they are involved in a different church experience, separated from the reality of what church is really going to be like when they are adults. Hence, they can lose connection with the true church experience, especially since the focus of children's church is often on catering to them and that focus extends to their teen years.

In this context, when the church stops catering to them as young adults and asks them to begin serving, the adult church experience does not match the entertaining church experience they have been conditioned to anticipate. Furthermore, they may have made few to no close connections with adults at church because they never saw them. Thus, when they grow up and leave home, they find it easy to leave the church as well.

Please don't misunderstand. I am not opposed to children's church or to entertaining youth programs. I loved the years I spent as a youth director and all the fun, entertaining activities that went with it. I still love vacation Bible school, puppet shows, and church camp. However, along with these fun experiences, children and teens need to be given the opportunity to bond with the greater church family and feel as if they are an important part of the church. They need to be trained to serve so they don't grow up with a consumer mindset, thinking the church should cater to them. The small church is a wonderful place for children and teens to learn these lessons. It's a *good* thing that children of all ages are part of the worship service. And in most small churches, everyone is thrilled to hear toddler noises as part of the service. They're so glad to have children present, the noises are a blessing, and the noises can be enjoyed because small churches have a more relaxed atmosphere.

Relaxed Atmosphere

I recall a Sunday morning speaking engagement where the church service was planned out to the last minute. According to the schedule, I was supposed to stop speaking at 11:39 a.m. and had a strong impression that stopping one minute earlier or later would be frowned on. I know there are occasions when other activities follow and time is of the essence, such as at a conference when a plenary session must end at a certain time so the workshops can begin. Attendees expect conference directors to stay on schedule. However, this Sunday morning did not involve a conference. I also could understand the schedule rigidity if a television or radio broadcast was involved, but there was no such involvement. I did the best I could to conclude at 11:39, but that service was so severely scripted, I walked away wondering if they would make time for Jesus if he showed up in person and wanted to open the prayer altar for seekers. I also wondered if the "schedule police" would have arrived to arrest me if I violated the time requirement. As a pastor, I know that order is good and that there should be a balanced, planned order of service with time considerations for even the smallest congregations. However, we should never allow time constraints to overrule the movement of the Holy Spirit.

Fortunately, the small-church setting can offer an environment that allows for a more relaxed atmosphere that gives people the opportunity to engage with the service on a more personal level. In a healthy small church, it's OK if the service ends a bit late—or early—and there are usually no schedule police ready to pounce if the speaker stops at 11:49, instead of 11:39. As the Top 10 list indicates, it's OK to interrupt the song service with a testimony, even if it does add time to the worship service, and the more testimonies the better. It's also OK to ask for an unplanned, special prayer during the pastoral prayer time, and the church body will gather around the one who needs that prayer.

Furthermore, special events, such as Christmas programs, are usually full of bloopers, and that's what makes them so great. Recently at a small church, a newlywed couple in their eighties lit the Advent candles together. The husband had recently accepted Christ as his Savior, and the wife had recommitted her life to the Lord. The couple had joined the church and had become a big part of church life. They were delighted to share a Christmas reading and light the Advent candles. However, it became a challenge for the husband to remember that he was supposed to light the pink candle that week. Before it was over, he had all the purple candles lit, but not the pink one.

The pastor, sitting on the front pew, discreetly said "Light the pink candle," because even in a small church, you don't want to just blurt out the correction. The pastor's wife kindly chimed in.

Since the man was hard of hearing, he didn't hear the pastor or his wife. So a church member with a bolder voice said, "Pink candle!"

That's when the man's wife looked at her husband and openly said, "You lit the wrong candle. It's supposed to be the pink one." There was no option to whisper, because he wouldn't hear her.

"Oh!" he said. Then he finally lit the pink candle and snuffed out one of the purple candles.

As they completed their task, the wife looked at the audience and said, "Well, we didn't do that very well." The whole congregation laughed. Such a relaxed atmosphere in a small church is part of what makes it so appealing for many people. In a healthy small church, everyone who wants to take part is allowed to take part, and human flaws, even in Christmas programs, are expected and celebrated.

Up-Front Opportunities for Those Still Learning

The relaxed atmosphere also sets the stage for people who are still learning to teach, preach, or musically contribute. In a small church, the goal is usually not a perfect presentation, but a perfect love for the Lord and his people. So if you stop and restart your special song, nobody cares, and sometimes the person who stops and restarts is not a beginner. Small-church congregants are usually just glad someone is willing to share a vocal or instrumental number, and they embrace the experience for the journey and the blessing. Furthermore, many preachers testify to sharing their first sermons in a small congregation. The sermons may have been only a few minutes long and may have been awkward, but their church family gathered around them at the end of each service and cheered them on. Likewise, those interested in teaching will find an open opportunity to do so and will be given the grace to struggle a bit as they learn.

You *Won't* Get Lost in a Small Church

The Top 10 list states that you can't get lost in a small church, and many people love that about the building of a small church. There's not even an option to lose your way when looking for the bathroom. Often, it's just a "step or two down the short hallway." The truth is that a person would have to try hard to get lost in most small-church buildings.

However, even more importantly, you *won't* get lost in a small church. In a healthy small church, the pastor and lay leadership will make it a point to include any newcomers and make them feel welcome and part of the family. One woman chose to attend a small church simply because the people remembered her name. She was so astonished that the small-church pastor and laypeople called her by name and even reached out to her after her visit that she committed to attending the church. I'm reminded of the lyrics to a 1980s pop song: "Sometimes you want to go / where everybody knows your name, / and they're always glad you came."[12]

We live in a world where many people feel they are just a number, and they enjoy the personal touch of walking into a small church, knowing they won't get shuffled aside or fall through the cracks. Quite the contrary, if regular attendees miss church without reporting in, there may be a churchwide alert to find them or at least find out if they are OK. When a small church is functioning as it should, people are as concerned about a missing regular attendee as they would be about a missing family member who didn't show up at the weekly family meal. Consequently, somebody in the church may text the missing person, get the scoop, and often have a report on the person's absence during the open prayer-request time. This is the reason many small-church attendees will report in with someone if they are going to miss church, just as they would let a family member know they weren't going to be at the family meal.

Your prayer requests also won't get lost in a small church, and they are usually listed in the church bulletin. As a matter of fact, if you don't want your upcoming colonoscopy to be on the bulletin prayer list, you better let the pastor know. In smaller congregations, health-care prayer requests are often openly shared, just as they are in a fully functioning immediate family. People know each other well and share each other's burdens.

Granted, in our consumer culture, there are people who want to maintain anonymity in church attendance. They want to slip into the back pew, enjoy the worship service, and slip away with no commitment to serve and without anyone knowing they were there. While this is a definite issue in our culture, not everyone wants this anonymous church experience. Plenty of people still want the close bond a small church offers; they still want to feel that somebody cares for them enough to text them when they don't show up at church. They want to know that they *won't* get lost in their small church.

Celebrate the Advantages

Despite the consumer culture, there are people in your community who will respond to your small church and who will appreciate your church's advantages. The statistics featured in this chapter don't lie. They speak the bold truth that small churches are making a great impact on our culture. Small churches aren't failures because they are small; they successfully serve as individual threads in the fabric of our culture. These truths should be celebrated!

As already stated, I have repented of thinking that the goal is to get small churches to change into something they are not. However, that does not mean that small-church attendees should celebrate how great their small churches are to the extent that they become satisfied attendees with an inward focus, as discussed in chapter 1. "The harvest truly is plentiful, but the laborers are few" (Matt. 9:37, NKJV). Therefore, I am praying that recognizing the advantages of small churches will be an encouraging experience that will prompt small-church pastors and lay leaders to "send out laborers into His harvest" (v. 38, NKJV) and to do an even greater job at what the statistics indicate they are already doing—reaching their communities for Christ. Small-church pastors and lay leaders should never underestimate the power of their small church to do great things for the kingdom of God. Thus, three good small-church goals are as follows:

- To become a healthy spiritual family that impacts the community and reaches people who don't know Christ
- To place a greater emphasis on spiritual growth and relational growth and let the numerical growth bloom from these strong foundations (see chaps. 3, 4, and 6)
- To follow the New Testament church model[13] and seek God's will in planting another small church if the Lord leads or the church outgrows its building

Please know that the purpose of this book is not to give instructions in church planting. However, you will find more information about planting a Kangaroo Church in chapter 6.

The Challenges

While we have celebrated the advantages of small churches in this chapter, it is important to also recognize that small churches can face some challenges that must be overcome. Even though small churches do have fantastic advantages, and many small churches are making a greater kingdom impact than they realize, it would be a significant lack of insight not to honestly address the challenges small churches face that may impact their health. The consumer culture is but one of those challenges. Chapters 7 and 8 examine additional small-church challenges.

Whatever the issues may be, it's also important to remember that speaking negatively about the church because of any perceived issues is not a healthy avenue to overcoming the problems. If there are issues, the first step to recovery is admitting there is a problem. Therefore, while small-church pastors and lay leaders should recognize and admit any problems, that doesn't give license to negativity or speaking death over the church. Rather, it's a place to say, "We are seeing that we do have a problem or two, but we believe the Lord can deliver and move our church to health so that we can make a greater impact on our community." In the process, the focus should be on getting the small church healthy so it can do what it does best—thrive as a close-knit family that welcomes new family members with open arms.

"As a prisoner for the Lord, then, I urge you to live a life worthy of the calling you have received. Be completely humble and gentle; be patient, bearing with one another in love. Make every effort to keep the unity of the Spirit through the bond of peace" (Eph. 4:1-3).

PAUSING TO PLAN

- Each participant should choose at least one key concept he or she found especially meaningful or applicable to

your church. As a group, discuss all the key concepts each participant has chosen.

- Reflect on the negative messages the consumer culture sends to small-church lay leaders and pastors. Answer these two questions: How has the negative message affected our attitude toward our small church? How has the negative message affected our attitude toward the value of our ministry in the church?
- What are the advantages specific to our small church?
- What specific ways can we start communicating with our congregants about our church's importance and its potential impact on the world?

Top 10 Advantages of Church Attendance

10. Fellowship and friendships
 9. A place to belong
 8. A spiritual family who cares
 7. A pastor who cares
 6. Accountability
 5. Discipleship
 4. The power of corporate worship
 3. Prayer support
 2. Biblical guidance
 1. God's anointing on church services

"Where two or three gather in my name,
there am I with them" (Matt. 18:20).

THREE

Reaping the Growth Spiritually
Entire Sanctification

●———————●

Now may the God of peace Himself sanctify you completely; and may your whole spirit, soul, and body be preserved blameless at the coming of our Lord Jesus Christ.

—1 Thess. 5:23, NKJV

Spiritual Growth Overcomes Consumer Impulses

The main solution to the consumer culture's impact is spiritual growth and formation and God's powerful anointing on a church. There is no depth of consumer impulse that can overcome the human heart's cry to have intimacy with God. The consumer culture has convinced people that material acquisition is the answer to their internal needs, but no amount of consumer gain can compete with the felt presence of God in a church with people whose primary goal is to seek him. Therefore, seek God's anointing and his felt presence for your church. It is that anointing that will propel a church to spiritual victory, cause people to return to the small church, and make a lasting difference in lives, both young and old. There is no program any church of any size can offer that can compete with the holy presence of a holy God. If church attendees experience only one thing, and that one thing is encountering God's presence, then the purpose of that church is fulfilled.

This powerful anointing is, unfortunately, not always a given in today's church world. Too many times the church has succumbed to the spirit of material consumerism and has forgotten that God calls us to be immersed in his Spirit, both privately and corporately. Matthew 18:20 states, "For where two or three gather in my name, there am I with them," and Christ's presence is what matters most. When the focus of a church shifts from seeking God for who he is and being satisfied with his presence to wondering how many more programs it can create to attract more people, the church will lack the powerful anointing that the old-timers once testified to.

That powerful anointing is available today. And it is that anointing that will propel a church to spiritual victory. It is that anointing that will cause people to return to your church. It is that anointing that will make a lasting difference in lives, both young and old.

The glory of God cannot be replicated, fabricated, or conjured through a perfect performance. God pours out his anointing, not because the performance is perfect, but because the worship is authentic. Those who have experienced his glory and anointing know the difference between his felt presence and emotional hype. Either he pours out his Spirit or he does not. And church pastors and lay leaders bear the responsibility of setting the atmosphere that is conducive to God's glory falling, and that glory leads to lasting spiritual growth that is foundational to sustainable church growth.

This is the stuff that revival is made of. And I believe that God is calling the small church to be the conduit of that revival. If small-church pastors and lay leaders will reject the lie that their church is insignificant; embrace the truth that their church is part of a mighty army that wields major impact; and commit to regular, powerful corporate prayer for revival, then God will hear. He will answer. And we will see a widespread revival that rivals those of old.

Only through the sanctifying power of the Holy Spirit in the lives of consecrated believers can God's glory be manifested. The message of entire sanctification and the baptism with the Holy Spirit must not be minimized to words on paper. It must be embraced, experienced, and powerfully lived out in the lives of ministry leaders so that church attendees will be inspired to allow the Lord to spiritually transform them from a cultural me-focus to the scriptural Christ-focus.

When a pastor boldly embodies a powerhouse experience with the Lord that produces powerful preaching and powerful love for God's people, the congregation will refocus on God's higher calling and regain the anointing that our culture so desperately needs to experience. Out of the overflow of God's supernatural power and direction, a small church can and will experience healthy spiritual growth that produces new converts, the re-commitment of souls who have strayed, and established believers perpetually going deeper in the Lord.

The small-church pastor fills a highly influential spiritual role. The closeness to church members can produce a greater potential for the hands-on discipleship and spiritual guidance that Christ exhibited. When pastors and lay leaders focus first on spiritual growth in their personal lives, they will see growth that reaps significant results in all aspects of ministry because the growth will happen within the outflow of their own spiritual depths that comes from the hand of God.

Before an airplane takes off, a recorded message instructs passengers what to do in case the air pressure in the cabin declines. Oxygen masks will fall from above, and passengers are advised about how to place the oxygen masks on their faces. They are also told that guardians of children are to place their own oxygen masks on before putting them on the children. This requirement may seem wrong because an adult should put the child's safety ahead of his or her own. However, the child will be better served if their guardian can breathe. If the guardian passes out while trying to secure the child's mask, then the child will be without his or her provider and protector.

The same concept applies to pastors and lay leaders. As church leaders, we must tend to our own spiritual growth first. If church leaders are spiritually waning from a lack of "breathing in the presence of the Holy Spirit," then they are of less help to those they are serving. Without the regular pivotal time of being still and knowing that he is God (Ps. 46:10), we can lose our spiritual stability, and before we know it, we are being "[conformed] to the pattern of this world," rather than being "transformed by the renewing of [our minds]" through the presence of the Holy Spirit (Rom. 12:2).

At this point, the consumer-culture mentality can creep in and compromise spiritual integrity. Spiritual compromise is a subtle rebellion that appears as a place of comfort because it avoids the challenge of wholehearted commitment and the scandal of outright iniquity. However, while Satan wants our compromise, God wants our consecration. The consumer mindset is not a place of consecration to the Lord. It is fueled by self-centeredness, with a focus on "I rule! I want to be served, and I want it my way," which is the essence of carnality. However, Ephesians 5:18 says that we are to "be filled with the Spirit," and Hebrews 12:29 states, "For our 'God is a consuming fire.'" Entirely sanctified people are not consumed by the consumer culture. They are consumed by the Holy Spirit. Hence, it is of greatest importance that pastors and lay leaders commit to soul care and tend the fires of their hearts first to make certain their own motives are the motives of Christ.

With that said, if there is ever an hour when church pastors and lay leaders need to refocus not only on experiencing entire sanctification but also on teaching this biblical truth, it is now. If we are to impact our culture for Christ through his power, the holiness message of entire sanctification must not be marginalized, minimized, or explained away. The holiness message must be centralized, maximized, and explained clearly.

Entire Sanctification

Sanctification is a biblical concept that must not be ignored. God's sanctifying grace gives us the power to live a life pleasing to him, a life victorious over willful, known sin. Even though the concept is biblical, and the Bible calls us to "abstain from every form of evil" (1 Thess. 5:22, NKJV) and "not let sin reign in your mortal body" (Rom. 6:12, NKJV), it is perplexing how many Christians claim to have sin in their lives and act as if living for Christ and living in sin are simultaneous conditions the Bible supports because of God's grace. However, the Bible in no way supports the idea of God's grace enabling a lifestyle of sin, of a person willfully and knowingly participating in sin with a cursory "Sorry, Lord" at the end of each day. "Grace" that excuses and enables sin is codependency that leads to spiritual irresponsibility. True grace empowers full repentance that leads to righteousness.

God's grace cannot be earned, but it also must not be trampled. Trampling God's grace can be spiritually devastating, causing people to never experience what Romans 6 so clearly articulates, the freedom from sin found in living the Spirit-filled life. The message that being a Christian involves daily sinning—always asking forgiveness, but never truly repenting—sets up people for a lifetime of spiritual failure, heartache, and sin's bitter consequences. The message that being a Christian involves living a holy life, always resisting sin, never embracing it, leads people to a lifetime of spiritual victory, a clean heart, and the Lord's blessed anointing.

Unfortunately, when people are taught that Christians sin every day, they will do exactly that. They will embrace sin as a way of life, and the consequences of those sins may derail them for life. God calls all Christians to live a holy life (1 Pet. 1:16). The last thing people need to believe is that the Holy Spirit can't empower them to live above willful, known sin. Many people are willing to accept the miraculous gift of salvation through faith in Christ, known as initial sanctification, but believe that the same God who has the power to save them does not have the power to deliver them from a lifestyle of sin.

Consequently, such passages as 1 John 1:8 have been taken out of context to support Christians knowingly living in sin. Verse 8 states, "If we claim to be without sin, we deceive ourselves and the truth is not in us." However, this verse in no way should be used to support willful, known sin in the lives of Christians, because the following verse clearly indicates that "if we confess our sins, he is faithful and just and will forgive us our sins and purify us from *all unrighteousness*" (v. 9; emphasis added). A person cannot live in sin and at the same time be purified from *all unrighteousness*. Thus, verse 8 is not speaking of people who have already repented of their sins and made Christ Lord of their lives; the verse is speaking of people who have sin in their lives but are in denial about it, refusing to fully repent.

The claim that the Lord will purify from *all unrighteousness* reverberates with the understanding that the Lord has the power to purify the soul as well as give people the power to devote the body to acts of righteousness, not unrighteousness. First Corinthians 6:19-20 states, "Do you not know that your bodies are temples of the Holy Spirit, who is in you, whom you have received from God? You are not your own; you were bought at a price. Therefore honor God with your bodies." Given God's power to fully cleanse the whole person and the scriptural call to use our bodies to honor God, the claim that people have no choice but to sin and that the sin won't affect their souls or their standing with the Lord carries no credence. We know this interpretation is the correct one because 1 John 3:6-10 further states,

No one who lives in him keeps on sinning. No one who continues to sin has either seen him or known him.

Dear children, do not let anyone lead you astray. The one who does what is right is righteous, just as he is righteous. The one who does what is sinful is of the devil, because the devil has been sinning from the beginning. The reason the Son of God appeared was to destroy the devil's work. No one who is born of God will continue to sin, because God's seed remains in them; they cannot go on sinning, because they have been born of God. This is how we know who the children of God are and who the children of the devil are: Anyone who does not do what is right is not God's child.

In other words, when you are truly committed to Christ, you stop dallying with the devil.

First Thessalonians 5:23 further states, "Now may the God of peace Himself sanctify you completely; and may your whole *spirit, soul, and body* be preserved blameless at the coming of our Lord Jesus Christ" (1 Thess. 5:23, NKJV; emphasis added).

Given these passages and many like them, it is important for pastors and lay leaders to teach that a sanctified life, free of a lifestyle of willful, known sin, is not only a scriptural directive but also humanly possible, not from our own efforts, but through the indwelling power of the Holy Spirit. Furthermore, it is through the entire sanctification experience that people will have the Spirit-filled power and insight to act in alignment with the Lord's leading, rather than cave to the "me first" impulse the consumer culture appeals to.

In past decades, the experience of entire sanctification was, at times, taught in a way that was not wholly balanced or biblical. A person was instructed to "make a second trip to the altar" to experience entire sanctification as a point of spiritual arrival. Once the person had experienced entire sanctification, he or she was somehow supposed to be without struggles, infirmities, or issues, and if that person had struggles, infirmities, or issues, he or she was not entirely sanctified.

Legalism developed in this context. Being entirely sanctified meant that people obeyed the rules, and the rules ruled. Although Christ did say "If you love me, you will keep my commandments" (John 14:15, ESV), the impetus for keeping the commandments is supposed to be a love relationship with Christ, not a perfectionistic relationship with the rules. Furthermore, the long list of extraneous rules many times had no clear warrant from Scripture. For instance, in the mid-twentieth century, some people taught that if a woman wore open-toed shoes, it was sinful. Such an idea is now hilariously ridiculous, but they were serious about the sinful-toes business. Moreover, well-meaning saints would even "test" people to see if they were really sanctified, which was essentially abuse in the name of "holiness."

These sorts of abuses, legalistic views, and even loopy definitions of sanctification have caused people to deny or diminish the experience and, sometimes, even avoid the topic when preaching or teaching. However, sound holiness teaching is neither loopy nor legalistic, but a balanced message of God's Spirit and complete love filling the hearts of consecrated believers committed to obeying a holy God. True holiness of heart is characterized by the presence of God's perfect love expelling all willful, known sin. Holiness teaching that focuses solely on love and ignores the call to "abstain from all appearance of evil" (1 Thess. 5:22, KJV) results in a low-standard perspective that believers can do whatever they want to do if they "feel the love." Holiness teaching that focuses solely on "abstain[ing] from all appearance of evil" but ignores the call to Christlike love results in a legalistic mentality that is more concerned about following the rules than showing God's love. We serve a God who told us not only to "be holy" but also to "love one another."

Given these thoughts, if churches are going to plow through the consumer culture to victory, we must embrace the only power that will bring that victory—the *cleansing* power of the Holy Spirit in the lives of *consecrated* believers. With that said, the entire sanctification experience involves much more than a second trip to the prayer altar that establishes a static point of spiritual arrival that can lead to legalism. Quite the contrary, entire sanctification encompasses a point in time, a process, and a practice.

Point in Time

Entire sanctification is a point in time that embodies two sides—our side and God's side. Our side is *consecration*; God's side is *cleansing*. When we consecrate ourselves to the Lord, he cleanses our hearts of the carnal consumer me-focus, the root of sin, and replaces it with a Christ-focus, the source of victory. Only when we fully get over ourselves can we fully embrace the mind of Christ.

Some Christians testify that this point of consecration comes after realizing that even though they have accepted Christ as Savior, they still want to control and rule their lives. They are thus engaged in an internal struggle against the Holy Spirit's wooing to relinquish all to him. At the same time, the Holy Spirit reveals to them that they are lacking a spiritual power to live victoriously over willful, known sin. We read about such a struggle and the victory over it in Galatians 5:16-18 when Paul states, "So I say, walk by the Spirit, and you will not gratify the desires of the flesh. For the flesh desires what is contrary to the Spirit, and the Spirit what is contrary to the flesh. They are in conflict with each other, so that you are not to do whatever you want. But if you are led by the Spirit, you are not under the law."

Scripture is clear then that there is deliverance from the me-focused "desires of the flesh" that can entice the unconsecrated Christian to live outside the will of the Lord, against the scriptural calling to live a holy life. "But if we walk in the light, as he is in the light . . . the blood of Jesus, his Son, purifies us from all sin" (1 John 1:7). If God's power was miraculous enough to raise Christ from the dead, it is miraculous enough to raise us from the depths of sin to a life of holiness. As Scripture indicates, the Lord's intent is to purify us from all willful, known sin through the power of the Holy Spirit alive and active in the hearts of consecrated believers, not to leave us trapped in sin so that we never completely experience abundant life. "I have come that they may have life, and that they may have it more abundantly" (John 10:10b, NKJV). A life of sin is not abundant.

The Old Testament book of Joshua provides an example of full consecration to the Lord. The children of Israel had been wandering in the wilderness for forty years. However, in the Lord's timing, they prepared to cross the Jordan River to the promised land. In Joshua 3:5, "Joshua told the people, 'Consecrate yourselves, for tomorrow the LORD will do amazing things among you.'" So the people consecrated themselves to the Lord and thus became the vessels of his bidding to cross the Jordan River.

Crossing the Jordan River is symbolic of leaving a life of spiritual wandering to a spiritual life "flowing with milk and honey," through the Holy Spirit's power (5:6). The children of Israel had to once and for all divorce themselves from the fear and lack of commitment to the Lord that their ancestors had allowed to steal their spiritual victory. However, they had to step into the waters of the Jordan River for it to part. There was no way they could cross the Jordan unless it parted. In an act as miraculous as the parting of the Red Sea, the Lord parted the Jordon, and the children of Israel at long last entered the promised land.

So it is with us as we divorce ourselves from our fear and lack of commitment to the Lord and consecrate ourselves to him so that we become a vessel of his bidding to cross our own

Jordan River into the promised land. Just as the Lord parted the Jordan River for the people of Israel, so does he remove the obstacle of our own carnal, self-centeredness that flows through the center of our hearts to give us spiritual freedom in the promised land. The truth is that a Spirit-filled cleansing power awaits the consecrated heart. When we stop seeking God in a consumer mindset—only for what he can give us—and start seeking God simply to know him, we come to understand consecration.

Process

Our hearts are like an internal house. When we repent and accept Christ as our Savior, he becomes a resident in our house. From that moment, we experience a time of growth—initial sanctification—as already mentioned. However, for most people, they are still the president of the house and still hold the master key to every room. Full consecration happens when we relinquish the master key to Jesus, allow him to move from becoming our resident to becoming our president, and commit our lives to living a holy life through his power. The minute we hand him the master key to our internal house, we experience entire sanctification, and a new process of growth begins. Christ then has full control of our lives and full right-of-way to every room in our internal house, including the messed-up basement, the family skeletons stacked in the attic, and the guilt room we have no use for.

While entire sanctification is a point in time, it is also a point of beginning, not a point of arrival. When entire sanctification is taught as a static point of spiritual arrival, it sets up Christians for defeat as they stretch for a perfectionistic experience that leaves no room for additional growth, deliverance, and repentance, if needed. Such an "I've arrived" mindset not only is prideful but also denies the need for the Lord to go through our internal house, one room at a time, to purge and deliver and mature us so that we can continue to grow to be more like him.

Once the children of Israel crossed the Jordan River into the promised land, the Lord instructed them to purge the land of pagan influence, beginning with Jericho (Josh. 6). Likewise, the sanctification journey involves the Lord's instruction for us to purge our lives of anything he shows us that is not pleasing to him. In the initial moment of entire sanctification, that purging involves God's calling us to quit willfully and knowingly sinning. However, the process of his refining fire becomes a lifelong journey.

Psalm 19:12-13 states, "But who can discern their own errors? Forgive my hidden faults. Keep your servant also from willful sins; may they not rule over me." This passage echoes with the same theme as Romans 6, which calls believers not to allow sin to reign over them. This passage also points to a need for forgiveness for hidden faults. Hidden faults are not willful sins that a believer knowingly commits daily. They are areas of our lives that we do not see that may need to be confessed and forgiven, such as an unholy attitude that slowly creeps in. Hidden faults can also be emotional woundedness, personality infirmities, or issues from our childhood or our past that cause us to spontaneously act out in ways that are not pleasing to the Lord. Deliverance and healing from these hidden faults are what the sanctification process is about. The Lord will show us these issues, often one at a time, as he works with us to bring about our spiritual and emotional health.

Just as physical wounds heal over time, so the Lord can and will also heal emotional wounds over time as we journey with him in the process following entire sanctification. Mature Christians who fully understand sanctification as a process will commit to allowing younger Christians, still new in their sanctification journey, to have the time to grow and find deliverance through God's grace. All hidden faults are not and will not be removed in a flash, especially those rooted in emotional wounds. These types of wounds don't usually happen overnight, and it can take years to unravel the emotional knots that have been tightly tied through many years of exposure to unhealthy or toxic situations, especially in childhood.

Childhood wounds are like a cup of sand that has been dumped into a gallon of new paint. When sandy paint is rolled onto the wall of a house, the sand will dry into the paint. Removing the sand from the wall will involve removing the contaminated paint and replacing it with pure paint. As part of the process following entire sanctification, the Lord is committed to scouring each of our sand-laden walls with his purifying Holy Spirit and replacing the sandy paint with pure paint. However, the person must remain surrendered to God's will as God accomplishes what can seem to be a painful, time-consuming task. The result will be a healthy person who can function in victory, not from his or her own power, but because of the delivering power of the Holy Spirit through the sanctification process.

The sanctification process can also include negative behavioral patterns passed down from parents to children. These behavioral patterns can likewise be so engrained in the minds of the believer that it takes the Holy Spirit's coaching and guidance to unravel over time what took many years to establish as daily behavior. Negative behavioral patterns can take the form of such things as addictions, habitual criticism, codependency, living in conflict, and control issues rooted in a fear of "life getting out of control as it did in childhood." Part of the sanctification process involves the Lord making us aware of such behavioral patterns, leading us to ask forgiveness and, ultimately, requiring us to repent, which means stopping the behavior. Many people also find balanced Christian counseling beneficial as they progress in the process toward wholeness, healing, and deliverance.

Furthermore, many mature Christians who are fully consecrated to the Lord testify that the sanctification process also engages the times they miss the mark and spontaneously say or do something that grieves the Holy Spirit. Missing the mark without willful intent is not the same as perpetually and knowingly living in sin without true repentance, which is what 1 John 3:9 references: "No one who is born of God will continue to sin." The idea of "continu[ing] to sin" includes a perpetual state, a daily lifestyle. However, even though a person may unintentionally say or do something that is not in alignment with the biblical truths, that issue must not be excused or ignored. First John 2:1-2 states, "My dear children, I write this to you so that you will not sin. But if anybody does sin, we have an advocate with the Father—Jesus Christ, the Righteous One. He is the atoning sacrifice for our sins, and not only for ours but also for the sins of the whole world." The clear goal from Scripture is that Christians will not sin; however, if there is a moment in time when a sanctified Christian falls short, the Holy Spirit's conviction will then be swift and powerful, and the consecrated believer's repentance will be swift and earnest. Thus, the saints of God who love him more than their own lives testify to immediately confessing and repenting of that thing that has grieved the Holy Spirit and praying that the Lord will give them the power not to repeat. When our holiness is rooted in God's perfect love, we will guard what we think, what we say, what we do because our primary desires are to please the Lord we love and to show his love to the people we influence.

Entire sanctification taught as a static point of arrival with no need for a perpetual process breeds accomplished maskers who are in denial about their own issues that others may be able to clearly see. This state of denial is in no way an honest testimony to the reality of God's dynamic sanctification process in the lives of consecrated believers. One of the greatest testimonies of God's existence is the person he has transformed into his image of grace and holiness, and living in denial about engrained issues derails such a testimony.

Practice

The practice of entire sanctification involves daily encountering the Lord. This daily encounter will include the Lord's ministering to us as we commit to soul care, and he nurtures us in his love. Furthermore, as we listen to him and bask in his presence, we receive the grace and power to find deliverance and overcome temptation. Therefore, the power to live a holy life does not come through a haphazard prayer life but through intentionally taking the time to daily center our lives on the Lord.

As a major element in the practice of entire sanctification, intentionally centering our lives on the Lord every day means carving out time to do so. A powerful prayer life will not happen by accident but by making time to make it happen. This is where so many people throw up their hands and say, "I just don't have the time." Ironically, those same people usually have plenty of time to sit for hours a week in front of the television. Either we have the time or the time has us, and the time will always have us if we don't seize it through God's power and allow him to order our time for us. The old hymn "My Wonderful Lord" contains some of my favorite lyrics: "I desire that my life shall be ordered by Thee, / That my will be in perfect accord / With Thine own sov'reign will, / Thy desires to fulfill, / My wonderful, wonderful Lord."[1] This verse echoes the message of Proverbs 3:5-7:

> Trust in the LORD with all your heart,
> And lean not on your own understanding;
> In all your ways acknowledge Him,
> And He shall direct your paths.
> Do not be wise in your own eyes;
> Fear the LORD and depart from evil. (NKJV)

Often, I pray, "Lord, order my life." The Lord has moved in answer to that prayer in amazing ways, but the most amazing way is in showing me where the time in my schedule lies for intentionally centering my life on him to regularly receive his sanctifying power through the avenue of prayer. Our daily spiritual goal should be to center ourselves in the Lord's presence and yield to his will so that he can order our lives and direct our paths. It is only in this place that we can effectively navigate our lives according to his purpose and his plan, which includes the departure from evil.

When we consider prayer, so many times we think of talking to God nonstop with our long list of items we need him to handle in the way we advise. However, part of true prayer is about God changing our hearts to align with his will, not our coercing God to align with our will. Even though we should lay our requests at his feet, waiting in God's presence to receive his anointing and direction is the greater part of prayer. Psalm 46:10 states, "Be still, and know that I am God." God speaks in a still, small voice, and we hear him best when we make ourselves still and small. One of the biggest temptations we must overcome is to be so busy we miss knowing that he is God because we don't make ourselves still and small, thus neglecting our personal prayer time. In such a hustle and bustle of daily activities, we can assume that knowing *about* God is the same as knowing God. When we substitute knowing God with knowing *about* God, we lose intimacy with God. A loss of intimacy with God means a loss of spiritual power. However, the power is in the hour. The more time spent with Christ, the greater the spiritual power.

The inverse is also true. The neglect of personal prayer leads to spiritual weakness. Spiritual weakness leads to lower temptation resistance. Lower temptation resistance leads to spiritual failure. The power of personal prayer must never be undervalued or overlooked. It is our spiritual lifeline. And following that regular encounter with the Lord, we must remain with the Lord in the secret place of our hearts because that is where refuge is found and strength and security abound. Psalm 91:1 speaks a great truth: "He who dwells in the secret place of the Most High shall abide under the shadow of the Almighty" (NKJV).

The practice of entire sanctification means daily being filled with the Holy Spirit and dying to self. Paul states, "I die daily" (1 Cor. 15:31*b*, NKJV). Thus, the theme verse of the entirely sanctified believer is Galatians 2:20: "I have been crucified with Christ and I no longer live, but Christ lives in me. The life I now live in the body, I live by faith in the Son of God, who loved me and gave himself for me." However, we must be still for the fill. The infilling of the Holy Spirit doesn't happen in a flurry of activities. It happens as we "be still" and know that he is God and wait for his Spirit to work (Ps. 46:10*a*). James 4:8*a* states, "Come near to God and he will come near to you." We are each as close to God as we invest the time to be.

A key factor in having a powerful prayer life is living a righteous private life. "The prayer of a righteous person is powerful and effective" (James 5:16*b*).

Furthermore, regularly reading the Word of God and church attendance undergird the practice of entire sanctification. Being set apart for God and for the things of God is an element of entire sanctification. The practice of reading the Bible and attending church support the idea that we are "a chosen people, a royal priesthood, a holy nation, God's special possession, that [we] may declare the praises of him who called [us] out of darkness into his wonderful light" (1 Pet. 2:9). Hebrews 4:12 states, "For the word of God is alive and active. Sharper than any double-edged sword, it penetrates even to dividing soul and spirit, joints and marrow; it judges the thoughts and attitudes of the heart." The act of regularly basting our minds in the Word of God provides an avenue for the Lord to encourage us but also to show us our hidden faults and areas we need him to purge. Romans 12:2 speaks of being "transformed by the renewing of your mind." The Bible is the inspired Word of God, providing wisdom and truth that renew the minds of those who feast on its riches.

In addition, Scripture admonishes us to come together as the body of Christ. By doing so, we can encourage one another to persevere in our consecration to the Lord, to not give up, and to commit to acts of righteousness. Hebrews 10:24-25 states, "And let us consider how we may spur one another on toward love and good deeds, not giving up meeting together, as some are in the habit of doing, but encouraging one another—and all the more as you see the Day approaching." There is power in being with God's people; the power does not come from the people, but from the presence of the Lord among believers. For the same Lord who admonishes us to not give up meeting together also states, "For where two or three gather in my name, there am I with them" (Matt. 18:20).

The Message of Holiness Is Not Outdated

The message of holiness is in no way outdated. God still calls us to embrace, live, and preach holiness. "Therefore, with minds that are alert and fully sober, set your hope on the grace to be brought to you when Jesus Christ is revealed at his coming. As obedient children, do not conform to the evil desires you had when you lived in ignorance. But just as he who called you is holy, so be holy in all you do; for it is written: 'Be holy, because I am holy'" (1 Pet 1:13-16).

When we speak of living a holy life, many Christian people claim they cannot achieve holiness, so they deny that living a holy life is possible. They think that the calling is impossible because they do not have the power to fulfill it. The truth is that human beings cannot live a holy life through their own effort and power. However, if living a holy life was not possible, the Lord would not call us to do so; the Bible would not repeatedly urge us to an experience that is impossible to live. Any consecrated believer can live a holy life through the indwelling presence of the Holy Spirit. Scripture speaks of a sanctifying grace that the Lord supplies for us to live a holy life: "He has saved us and called us to a holy life—not because of anything we have done but because of his own purpose and grace. This grace was given us in Christ Jesus before the beginning of time" (2 Tim. 1:9).

Despite the consumer culture's enticing message of material gain as a place of contentment, God's primary goal is for our spiritual wealth, not our material wealth. Material wealth can be gained through secular means. Spiritual wealth is only gained through consecration to the Lord, cleansing from the Lord, and communion with the Lord, and that cannot be fabricated.

Entirely sanctified people testify that when we walk with the Lord long enough and close enough, we discover he is enough. Thus, fully consecrated believers don't have a consumer-driven value system. They don't believe "It's all about me," and they don't expect the church to sing, "Have it your way" and "You rule!"[2]

The most important church growth is spiritual growth, and spiritual growth can't always be counted.

PAUSING TO PLAN

- Each participant should choose at least one key concept he or she found especially meaningful or applicable to

SMALL CHURCH, BIG IMPACT

your church. As a group, discuss all the key concepts each participant has chosen.

- What are two to three ways we can have a greater focus on spiritual growth in our own lives?
- What are two to three realistic ways we can hone our congregation's focus on intentional, personal spiritual growth?
- What plan can we put in place to regularly teach the concepts of entire sanctification?

Ten Great Reasons for a Relationship with Christ

- Adoption into the family of God
- Christ's spiritual guidance for life
- Joy that transcends circumstances
- Inner peace
- Love beyond comprehension
- Christ's comfort in sorrow
- His faithful friendship
- The forgiveness of sins
- Eternity in heaven
- Intimacy with God

"The Lord is not slow in keeping his promise, as some understand slowness. Instead he is patient with you, not wanting anyone to perish, but everyone to come to repentance" (2 Pet. 3:9).

FOUR

Reaping the Growth Spiritually
Evangelism

●————————————●

And behold, a man of Ethiopia, a eunuch of great authority under Candace the queen of the Ethiopians . . . had come to Jerusalem to worship [and] was returning. And sitting in his chariot, he was reading Isaiah the prophet. Then the Spirit said to Philip, "Go near and overtake this chariot."

So Philip ran to him, and heard him reading the prophet Isaiah, and said, "Do you understand what you are reading?"

—Acts 8:27-30, NKJV

Loving Soul Strategist

I'll never forget that flight. I was sitting by the plane's window, and a young man was sitting in the seat to my left. I felt the Lord nudging me to start a conversation with him, so I said something like, "Great weather, isn't it?" I have no memory of how it happened, but the conversation swiftly went into spiritual depths by the young man's own initiative. I never anticipated such a conversation when I had seen him boarding the plane.

But before it was over, I was openly talking Jesus with him at thirty thousand feet while I'm sure every passenger around us heard every word we were saying.

As things turned out, the young man had been in and out of intimate relationships with multiple women, and he had strayed far, far, far from the Lord. He explained that his grandfather was a pastor. I can imagine that his grandfather and grandmother both had been on their knees praying that somebody would intersect their grandson's path and tell him he needed to fully commit his life to the Lord. That somebody was me. I don't know what happened in that young man's life after his encounter with me, but I do know the Lord used me to speak to him about renewing his commitment to Christ. I also know my message was well received. I spent the next several months praying for that young man as the Lord brought him to mind.

When we talk in the church about sharing Christ, we often speak of the church reaching the lost as a sign of church health. However, it's important to remember that the church is made up of people. It's the people in the church who should be sharing Christ just as I did on that airplane. However, too many times, good church people, even church leaders, will sit through a whole plane trip, bus trip, or doctor's visit and never speak to the person sitting next to them or never engage anyone they meet in a conversation about Christ. Unfortunately, good Christian people who love the Lord may allow other forces to overtake their willingness to share their faith. Those forces might be fear and intimidation or a lack of awareness of how God is moving to orchestrate a conversation.

However, fear, intimidation, and a lack of awareness can be dramatically diminished when we realize how the Lord works in placing people in our lives. The Lord can arrange to open conversations about him if we stay tuned to him and recognize the clues. I believe that is exactly what happened with me and the young man on the airplane. The Lord purposefully placed him next to me and skillfully orchestrated a conversation that went into spiritual depths the young man needed to hear. When we understand this is a pattern the Lord uses, we can be empowered to know that we are participating with a loving Soul Strategist who is "not willing that any should perish" (2 Pet. 3:9, KJV). Theologically, Wesleyans believe that the Lord goes before each person in prevenient grace to bring about his or her salvation if he or she will accept him. With this understanding, we can trust him to alleviate any fear, ease intimidation, and through him, we can have the courage to simply engage in conversations about our faith, about what the Lord is doing in our lives, about how Christ has brought us freedom and joy. All the Lord asks is that we be willing to partner with him to share our story for his glory.

I'm reminded of a situation in Scripture where our loving Soul Strategist orchestrated a meeting between Philip and an Ethiopian eunuch for the purpose of Philip sharing the gospel with the eunuch. Acts 8:26-35 tells the story of the Lord leading Philip out into the desert at exactly the right time to intersect the Ethiopian. As it turns out, this man held a powerful position with the queen of Ethiopia, and his salvation would make a significant difference in spreading the gospel with those he influenced. Philip "just happened" to intersect the eunuch at the time he was reading Isaiah's prophetic passage about Christ, and Philip wasted no time obeying the Lord in striking up a conversation with him. The eunuch was ready to place his faith in Christ, and our loving Soul Strategist knew that.

If Philip hadn't obeyed the Lord in going into the desert and hadn't approached the man to start a conversation, but instead had shrunk away from the calling, I believe the Lord would have prompted someone else to speak to the eunuch because that's the stuff his prevenient grace is made of. Philip would have then missed out on an amazing opportunity to participate in God's soul strategy. Therefore, when we shrink away from the Lord's promptings to engage in conversations with people, we miss out on invigorating opportunities to witness people commit their lives to Christ. Thankfully, Philip didn't shrink from God's promptings. He approached the eunuch and simply said, "Do you understand what you are reading?" (v. 30). That's all it took. The loving Soul Strategist took over from there.

One of the characteristics of a healthy church is that the loving Soul Strategist is using attendees to draw people to him for salvation, recommitment, or deepening their faith. Christ's Great Commission to "go into all the world and preach the gospel" (Mark 16:15) still rings true today. If our culture is going to be changed for Christ, if revival is going to come, church people need to stop thinking, *"The church" needs to reach the lost,* or *The pastor needs to reach the lost,* and start thinking, *I need to reach the lost.* Church folks need to decide their desire to please the Lord and share their faith is greater than any fear or intimidation that Satan so skillfully uses to inhibit their testimony.

While all churches, no matter the size, are pivotal in leading people to salvation, I believe that God is calling small churches to be the conduit of an amazing outpouring of his Spirit that will impact the masses. And small churches can impact the masses because of their vast number. According to Vaters, "The Gospel of Jesus, packaged in Small Churches, is the most powerful force for goodness the world has ever seen. We don't need to build one more church building, gather for any more seminars or devise a new strategy in order to be ready for the greatest movement in history. We just need to say 'yes' to Jesus."[1] If attendees in each small church would commit to praying that their church would reach one person per year for Christ and commit to a personal willingness to be used of the Lord to fulfill that goal, as Philip did, millions would be converted, one person at a time. Our culture would then be revolutionized for the kingdom of God.

The soul that finds Christ in a small church is
as important to God as any other,
and God uses the small church for such souls
to find him—one at a time.

The Day of Pentecost

The story of Philip and the Ethiopian eunuch occurs numerous chapters after the Acts 2, day of Pentecost, event. Philip left a great evangelism effort among Samaritan villages to obey the Lord's direction to encounter one soul. His willingness to obey the Lord and to initiate a conversation with the Ethiopian eunuch is indicative of the power of the Holy Spirit that fell on the day of Pentecost and empowered the followers of Christ to share the gospel boldly and fearlessly.

Specifically, Peter stands out as the one who experienced a profound transformation through the infilling of the Holy Spirit. The same Peter who weakly allowed fear to drive him to deny Christ three times before Christ's crucifixion shines forth on the day of Pentecost as the one who boldly proclaims Jesus as the Messiah:

> Fellow Israelites, listen to this: Jesus of Nazareth was a man accredited by God to you by miracles, wonders and signs, which God did among you through him, as you yourselves know. This man was handed over to you by God's deliberate plan and foreknowledge; and you, with the help of wicked men, put him to death by nailing him to the cross. But God raised him from the dead, freeing him from the agony of death, because it was impossible for death to keep its hold on him. (Acts 2:22-24)

Peter is an example of the transformational effects of the baptism with the Holy Spirit.

Like Peter, people who have truly experienced entire sanctification will share their faith however the Lord leads. They will not cower in fear or believe that evangelism is only for pastors or people who are somehow superspiritual. If a church is not seeing converts and the people lack a passion for reaching the lost, the problem is a need for a renewed outpouring of the Holy Spirit on church attendees. The concepts of entire sanctification in chapter 3 present the remedy, and there is no shortcut. Out of this powerful sanctifying experience, people's hearts will be tuned to the heart of the Father, and they will hear his heart cry resounding from the throne of God that focuses the people of God on the mission of God—salvation through Jesus Christ our Lord. From that point, the Lord will orchestrate encounters between consecrated believers and people who need Christ, just as he did with me and the young man on the airplane, just as he did with Philip and the Ethiopian eunuch.

Evangelism University

One of the problems is that some church people have been conditioned to think that to effectively share the gospel, they must have special training. They must be graduates of Evangelism University, with a degree hanging on the wall to show that they are evangelism experts. Furthermore, they cringe in dread that someone will ask them a scriptural question they can't answer. However, anytime anyone asks me a scriptural question I don't have the answer to, I simply tell them, "I'll have to research that topic, and I'll get back with you." Then I go to my study Bible and, if needed, a commentary and dig out the answer. The "question police" have never once arrested me for making someone wait a few days while I researched an answer to a question.

Likewise, when I visit my doctor, I ask questions that the doctor tells me she will have to research to find the answers. The doctor soon provides the answers without ever being embarrassed or quitting her practice. Moreover, she never stops sharing with me the necessary steps for me to be healthy.

As Christians, we hold the answers to an even higher measure of health—spiritual health through a relationship with Jesus Christ. The last thing any of us needs to do is get intimidated and stop sharing our faith because someone may ask a question we have to go look up. Most Christians know enough through their own journey with the Lord to simply share what the Lord has done for them, and such a personal testimony can be powerful enough to make a lasting impact.

John 9 relates the story of a blind man who testified that Jesus restored his sight. Once the man was healed, his neighbors and acquaintances began to question him about how Jesus healed him. He explained that Jesus had spit in mud, placed the mud on his eyes, and told him to go wash in the Pool of Siloam. Soon the Pharisees got involved; they were especially concerned because Jesus healed the man on the Sabbath. They, too, asked the man how Jesus had restored his sight, and he repeated the story once more.

The Pharisees didn't believe the man had been blind and that Jesus had healed him, so they consulted his parents to confirm that he had been blind and to find out how he had regained his sight. *The parents caved to fear.* They confirmed that their son had been born blind and that now he could see. However, they pointed the Pharisees back to their son for any further answers "because they were afraid of the Jewish leaders, who already had decided that anyone who acknowledged that Jesus was the Messiah would be put out of [excommunicated from] the synagogue" (v. 22). The parents simply weren't willing to take a chance on witnessing to Christ's power, because it might cost them big. *Their own personal comfort outweighed what they knew to be the truth.*

At this point, the Pharisees repeated their questions to the man. That's when the man replied with the pivotal words, "One thing I do know. I was blind but now I see!" (v. 25). The man's testimony was enough. He didn't have all the answers, but he could testify to what Jesus had done for him. Likewise, we can testify to what Jesus has done for us—I was spiritually blind, but now I can see. And when the questions come, it's fine to say, "I don't have all the answers because we don't have to know all the answers; we simply must point people to *the answer*—our Lord and Savior, Jesus Christ."

Furthermore, too many times people are at a loss about how to share their faith, and they feel inadequate about doing so. However, they shortchange the power of the Holy Spirit to do most of the work for them. Like Philip and the Ethiopian eunuch, all we must do is be available. Philip didn't walk up to the Ethiopian's chariot with a big, memorized speech. All he did was follow the prompting of the Holy Spirit and said, "Do you understand what you are reading?" (Acts 8:30). When the eunuch responded, Philip was able to explain that the man was reading about Jesus. Never once does the passage indicate that Philip had some memorized script from his time at Evangelism University. It just all fell into place because the Lord wants people to know him, and he is willing to do most of the work to make that happen. We just need to be willing to ask a simple question or make some other generic comment that will lead to deeper, spiritual conversation, as it did with the young man and me on the airplane. I didn't quote Scripture to that young man. I just opened my mouth, and the Lord gave me the words.

Just as we don't have to earn our own salvation and we don't have to fill ourselves with the Holy Spirit, we also don't have to rely on ourselves to share the gospel. The one who brought about the plan of salvation is right there with us to share it as he opens doors for us to converse. When people fall prey to thinking they must have all the answers and a memorized script, they also fall prey to thinking they must share Christ in their own power. But the same Holy Spirit power that saves us and sanctifies us and keeps us is the same power that connects us in meaningful dialogue with people who need Jesus.

Please know that I am not opposed to degrees in apologetics or training in evangelism. By all means, the Lord can use these tools to reach people who don't know him. However, reaching the lost is God's heart cry, and he can and will use anyone who is willing to fulfill his mission, no matter that person's level of education or training, as indicated by his choice of disciples. He simply wants us to be willing.

Many times, we talk about evangelism as a matter of speaking to people we have never met and perhaps breaking out of our comfort zone. Although that can happen, this does not mean that every Christian every day should fulfill a pushy agenda to press strangers about their spiritual condition. A church attendee walked into my yard many years ago and began asking me pushy questions about my eternal destiny. Honestly, even as a devout Christian, I felt pressured and was relieved when she left. That whole approach is ineffective. There is a difference between accosting people we've never met about their eternal destiny and partnering with the loving Soul Strategist as he naturally opens conversational doors.

Although God does open doors for us to gracefully witness to strangers, many times evangelism happens with an acquaintance we see often or someone we know well. Dr. Scott Rainey tells the story of a wealthy uncle that had been in the family for quite some time. The extended family were Christians, and several family members had a burden for this relative. Dr. Rainey was one of the family members who carried a burden for him. After a season of praying for his uncle, Dr. Rainey knew the Lord was impressing him to speak to his uncle about his commitment to Christ. So the day came when he made an appointment for a visit with his uncle.

The uncle was glad to see Dr. Rainey. The generous man erroneously assumed that Scott had come to borrow money for a car, which was desperately needed, but Dr. Rainey assured him he had a different topic to discuss. At that point, he asked his uncle a few simple questions to see if his uncle was trusting Jesus as his Savior. The uncle was open to hearing the gospel story. At the end of Scott's sharing the story of God's saving work through Jesus's life, death, and resurrection, the uncle said, "Thank you for sharing this with me. No one has ever done that before." When Dr. Rainey asked his uncle if he would like to repent of his sins and put his trust in Jesus, his uncle said, "For ninety-one years, I have believed that everything happens by fate and cannot be controlled. You are asking me to change my views after ninety-one years. Can I have some time to think about this?" The Holy Spirit was at work. The Lord had been wooing him through his prevenient grace. Two weeks later, after another conversation about faith, Dr. Rainey's uncle repented of his sins and put his trust in Jesus as his Savior.

By the way, the first conversation ended with the uncle writing Dr. Rainey a check to buy a new SUV, which is not the normal outcome of an evangelism effort.[2] But it is a wonderful metaphor for the spiritual riches that the Lord bestows on people who are willing to join him in his plan to reach the lost.

There is an approach to evangelism that maintains that we need to witness to others about Christ with our lives and only use words "if necessary." Although it is true that a person living under the anointing of the Holy Spirit is a powerful testimony, and a person claiming to be a Christian while not living as such is a deterrent to any sort of evangelism, there does come a time when words need to be used. It can be very easy for a person afraid to share their faith to believe that if they faithfully live Christ, they're "off the hook" of using words.

Dr. Rainey's story is indicative that there does come a time when the Lord may lead us to use words to lead others to Christ. The uncle was surrounded by family members who were living Christ in front of him. The witness to Christ's saving power had been established. The time finally came when someone in the family needed to initiate a conversation with the uncle and provide a full explanation for how he, too, could commit his life to Christ. Dr. Scott Rainey obeyed the Lord to be the one to use words.

Focusing on What God Is Focused On

It's easy for small-church leadership to slip into focusing on how to get more people to attend the church so the church can be bigger, build on the higher attendance, and offer more programs to attract more people. In this mindset, the attention can shift from reaching the lost to "recycling Christians" who come from other churches. Of course, twenty dedicated Christians moving to a small church and committing to serve and give would indeed be a blessing to any small-church leadership. Don't turn them away!

However, both Christ's call to "go into all the world and preach the gospel" (Mark 16:15) and the call to preach the message of holiness must remain the church's primary aim. Spiritually effective churches, regardless of size, focus on sharing salvation, not coddling consumers. The people who don't know Jesus and find him through the small church's efforts will be the ones who will stay with that church. People who don't know Jesus and aren't attending church anywhere are not out church shopping. When they encounter the one who gives them their spiritual sight, they will also be more likely to be loyal to the church that pointed them to him.

One of the wonderful things about attending a small church is that attendees' prayer requests will be in the church bulletin. This is a good thing. However, so many times, most of the prayer requests center on physical issues—requests for healing and support—rather than on the salvation of souls. *There is nothing wrong with praying for physical healing!* Christ physically healed many people in his ministry, and he still does today. However, when a church also focuses on praying for the salvation of the lost, it shifts attention to the reason Christ came and aligns with God's mission of not wanting anyone to perish.

One of the things a church can do to shift the focus to reaching the lost is to have a published prayer-request list, available at church only, that features the initials of people who need Jesus, whether they are living in the area or not. The list should be updated and distributed regularly, perhaps as part of the weekly church bulletin. Every week, the church can join in prayer for the people on the salvation list. It's important to limit the names of the people to initials because one of them might attend church at some point, and that person might be uncomfortable if he or she happens to see his or her name on a salvation list.

Another way to shift a church's focus to reaching the lost is to have each willing attendee commit to praying for the salvation of someone he or she knows who needs Jesus. Each one will then write that person's name on two cards—one for home and one for church. Then he or she will tape one card to his or her bathroom mirror. Every time the participant looks in that mirror, he or she will pray for the salvation of the person named and pray that the Lord will put someone in that person's life with whom he or she can have a "Philip encounter." The card designated for church will be exchanged every week. During corporate prayer time, the participants will move to the front of the church and exchange cards with other participants. Then all participants will gather around the altar to pray for the names of the people on the cards. They can then keep the other person's card all week and pray for that name during the week. The next week, they will exchange names again. An added touch is for the pastor to light a candle or two (battery powered is best) during the prayer time to represent the people who need salvation.

Whatever idea you use, whether your own idea or one or both ideas above, expect the Lord to be pleased and to begin to anoint and move among the people. As he begins to move, invite people to publicly share their experiences in the corporate worship service. One of the advantages of a small church is that it's OK to testify in the Sunday morning worship service, and the more testimonies, the better. Many times, participants are so impacted by the alignment with the heart of God that they will be blessed and spiritually empowered in the process.

The church doesn't "need more people." People need more Jesus.

Remember, the focus on salvation is aligned with the heart of the Father, and he will build your church. Therefore, the names your church prays over should not be limited to just reaching the people close enough to attend your church. The motive should be the Lord's motive—the salvation of souls, no matter where they live. Therefore, some names on the list or the cards might belong to people who live out of town. Perhaps a grandparent might pray for the salvation of a grandchild who lives across the nation; and that grandchild might meet up with some person on an airplane who explains that the grandchild needs to devote his or her life to Christ, and the grandchild does exactly that.

The Churches across the Street

At the editing of this book, over three years have passed since we moved across the street from two small churches. In all that time, no representative from either church has walked across the street with a neighborhood welcome and an invitation to worship. No warm hello. No kind greeting. No interest in our family.

The point isn't that I'm sitting across the street bitterly pining away for these churches to reach out to me. After all, I'm an ordained elder in a different denomination and a pastor of a church. Furthermore, neither of the churches across the street represent a denomination I'd be interested in attending. The point is that they don't know that. For all they know, I could be a person who has never heard the message of salvation and who desperately needs Christ. I know enough about their theologies to say that they both believe in Jesus as Lord and Savior and can point the lost to him, but they have never even attempted to reach out to our family.

I will give these churches credit for having events outside their churches, as if they are attempting to "get outside the church walls." Recently, one of them had a Christmas event in the church parking lot. Last spring, one of them even had a tent revival in front of the church. My husband and I were outside working in the yard one evening while the revival service was in progress. By the time the service was over, I was watering a flower bed near the road. One of the revival attendees drove out of the driveway, about fifteen yards from where I was standing and never even looked at me.

To reiterate, I am not hurt or even irritated. But I am flabbergasted! This neglect simply cannot be—it must not be! I

now wonder if there may be other North American churches whose leaders are "not seeing" the people who are closest
to their church or home. If that is the case, I also wonder if
the Lord will one day hold those church leaders accountable
for their lack of sight. As mentioned earlier, a Wesleyan theological viewpoint embraces prevenient grace, a grace that goes
before in the process of God's wooing people to himself. So I
do believe that the Lord will "go before" even neglected church
neighbors to woo them to himself through other means. Nevertheless, church attendees are also called to share their faith.
The church exists, among other things, to point others to
Christ, and it is a haunting thing to witness a blatant lack of
outreach from such churches.

If all small-church pastors and lay leaders in North America would become aware of their communities and just reach
out to the homes or businesses that are closest to their churches
or their residences, I am convinced that we would see a massive increase in church attendance in North America. However,
these church pastors and lay leaders need to learn to focus on
how they can impact the lives of people right next door who
may not even know Jesus. The truth is small-church leaders
don't have to resort to fancy efforts to impact their communities. The opportunities for outreach are lying right outside the
doors of their churches and their homes.

I'm convinced the world can be saved using bananas! It's
as simple as, first, taking the time to build trust around the
neighborhood. And second, turning on the oven, salvaging
those browning bananas, making a batch of banana nut bread,
taking it to the neighbor, and saying, "Hi! Just wanted to let
you know we're glad you're across the street from our church

[or my house], and I'm just here to say, 'God bless you. Let us know how we can pray for you!'"

Christ calls us to "go into all the world and preach the gospel" (Mark 16:15).
"All the world" starts where your lawn ends. Befriend your neighbors, pray for them, "preach the gospel" by showing them Christ's love, and use words to evangelize them when the Lord so leads.

If small-church lay leaders and pastors will commit to building trust over time with the people near their churches or residences and then start baking some kind of bread or cookies for a few neighbors every month or every other month, I promise you, one of those neighbors will eventually show up at church and just might commit his or her life to the Lord. You may be thinking, *Everybody in our church, including the pastor and spouse, works full-time, and we just don't have the time.* In that case, never underestimate the power of the grocery-store bakery. Those people have the goods—cookies, cakes, brownies, and breads—all just waiting for small-church leaders to snatch them up and use them as an outreach tool.

PAUSING TO PLAN

- Each participant should choose at least one key concept he or she found especially meaningful or applicable to

your church. As a group, discuss all the key concepts each participant has chosen.

- Brainstorm about ways your church can focus on evangelism. Make a list of all ideas, no matter how out of reach an idea might seem. Sometimes an out-of-reach idea will lead to another great idea that is doable.

- Choose to implement two to three long-term ideas that will work in your ministry setting. Remember to avoid the temptation to go overboard and implement more ideas than there are resources and people to support. Keep the ideas doable and focused on what will be effective in your setting.

Top 10 Advantages of a Small-Church Potluck Meal

10. You can eat several desserts, and nobody cares.
 9. Somebody will bring homemade rolls that taste like angels made them.
 8. All the grandmas cook their "top secret" recipes that you can now find on the internet.
 7. You can learn six different ways to make English pea salad.
 6. The men are in a running competition to see who can smoke the best brisket, and the whole church is glad.
 5. When the aging "church queen" says grace, she prays for the missionaries, flood victims, and astronauts but forgets to pray for the meal—and everybody gets blessed.
 4. Even people who don't bring food are welcome to stay and eat.
 3. After the meal is over, people give you their leftovers.
 2. Visitors are treated like long-time friends.
 1. It's like a family reunion.

"Every day they continued to meet together in the temple courts. They broke bread in their homes and ate together with glad and sincere hearts" (Acts 2:46).

FIVE

Reaping the Growth Relationally

●━━━━━━━●

A dispute also arose among them as to which of them was considered to be greatest. Jesus said to them, "The kings of the Gentiles lord it over them; and those who exercise authority over them call themselves Bene-factors. But you are not to be like that. Instead, the greatest among you should be like the youngest, and the one who rules like the one who serves. For who is greater, the one who is at the table or the one who serves? Is it not the one who is at the table? But I am among you as one who serves."

—Luke 22:24-27

Family of God

One of the powerful aspects of small churches is the family bond that forms so that all who attend feel as if they are connected as brothers and sisters in Christ. In the healthiest small churches, there are no cliques and no attempts to leave people out. Rather, there is a spirit of inclusion and an unspoken invitation that says, "Come, join our family!"

This type of family bond and inclusion emerges out of the spiritual growth discussed in the previous two chapters, and it is a magnetic force that will compel people to come back to a church. There are unchurched people who long for the rich family connections that can happen at a small church. The need for a spiritual family connection is another factor that can outweigh the consumer mentality. However, such a family connection must be fostered by a pastor who intentionally leads the church more as a family than as an organization, purposefully fostering a family bond while committing to relational leadership.

Leading the Church as a Family

Small-church leaders should cherish and nurture the family connection that happens in the small-church setting. In a world where families are splintered and in turmoil, the family bond in a small church can be a healing balm and can even provide relationship connections that may rival those of a biological family. Thus, a small-church pastor should strategize to lead the church more as a family than as an organization that meets in a building. Granted, there are organizational elements and building needs that must be tended to in a church of any size. Board and committee meetings still need to happen. The annual pastor's report still needs to be submitted. Insurance coverage and building upkeep still need to be addressed. And financial reports still need to be prepared.

However, the overarching focus should be on the church as a family unit, with the building and organizational elements serving the family, not the family serving the building and organizational elements. In other words, the small church should not exist to keep up a building, although building upkeep is important. Rather, the building should serve as a place where church attendees can bond and grow as a family. When the focus shifts from the small church being a family with building

Five Advantages of a Good Small-Church Pastor

- The pastor is an up-close mentor and role model to children and youth.
- The pastor attends congregants' sporting events and special events.
- There is high-level accountability for both the pastor and congregants.
- You will receive lead-pastor visitations in the home and hospital and in times of grief.
- You can have a personal friendship with the pastor.

and organizational elements to the small church being a building and organization with a family element, then it's too easy to sacrifice relationships with people or leave people behind for the sake of the building or organization.

The thought process of sacrificing people for the building or organization goes something like this: *That single mom who comes every week has too many rowdy kids. Her kid who's in kindergarten even used a crayon to mark on the men's bathroom wall. We don't need people here who are going to leave marks on our building. That woman can't keep up with her kids, and it's not our job to help her. She had the kids. She should be responsible for them. If she can't do a better job of corralling her kids, then she doesn't need to attend our church.*

The thought process of leading the church as a family and truly valuing people as part of the family goes something like this: *I'm so glad that single mom who comes every week brings all five of her kids with her. They're a bit rowdy, but that's OK. Most of us were rowdy kids at one point. We love those kids just like they are. I noticed that one of her kids who's in kindergarten even marked on the men's bathroom wall with a crayon, but I lovingly coached him not to write on the church wall. I even got him to help me remove the crayon marks. When we were done, I realized we were going to have to paint that bathroom wall again, but that's OK. Building walls can be painted and repainted and will one day crumble, but the souls of that mother and her children will live forever. The poor mother gets very little support from the children's father, and our church folks should do a better job of helping her keep up with the kids when they come to church. I'd hate for her to get embarrassed over something one of her kids did and choose not to return to our church family. We wouldn't throw out our own children for marking up a bathroom wall, and we won't throw out her children for the same. She's part of our family, and that means something. That means we truly love her and her rowdy kids more than we love having a pristine building.*

When a small church has a core group of church leaders who embrace the concept that the church is a family first, the strength of that family bond can sustain the church through decades as one generation after another commits to that church as its spiritual family. Given these truths, there are key things a pastor can do to foster such a strong family environment:

- Publicly use family language as much as possible.
- Foster a family relationship connection.
- Encourage church members to care for each other as a family would.
- Use the family model for activities and events.

Publicly use family language as often as possible. Look for ways to integrate family language. For instance, instead of stating that the prayer altar is open during the pastoral prayer, state that it's a family prayer time around the altar. Instead of saying, "A member of our church needs prayer," say instead, "A member of our church family needs our prayers." Instead of saying, "Our church is having a potluck meal after the service Sunday morning," say, "Our church family is coming together for a potluck meal after church Sunday morning." Instead of saying, "We are so glad you have visited with our church today," say, "We are so glad you are visiting with our church family today." Adopt a theme song, such as "The Family of God." Sing it often. It's even OK to sing the church's family theme song every Sunday. Colleges and high schools may play and/or sing their school theme songs at every gathering. The repetition is a bonding element that will reinforce that the people present are not just attendees but valued members of a family. Such family language should be used as often as possible and should be viewed as a cornerstone of leading the small church as a family.

Foster a family relationship connection. Historically, people in churches of all sizes have called each other brother and sister. After all, we are "children of God . . . and joint-heirs with Christ" (Rom. 8:16-17, KJV); we are brothers and sisters in the Lord. Therefore, one of the ways to foster family connections is to encourage the congregation to address each other as brother and sister: Brother Abe, Sister Aida. Furthermore, a pastor should also publicly address church people as brother and sister to set an example to attendees to do likewise.

One of the great things about being in a small church is that everybody knows everybody else, and that factor lends itself to a family connection. However, sometimes friction can erupt because everybody knows everybody else. When people get closer to one another, they are more likely to see each other's faults and flaws. Then they can fall into the temptation of becoming critical of each other or getting on each other's nerves. However, the pastor who is leading the church as a family and fostering family relationships will say something such as, "Remember, she is your sister is Christ. Let's make a commitment to pray for her and ask the Lord to help her overcome." Such a pastor understands that if a brother or sister has issues that are "worthy of criticism," he or she is more worthy of prayer and that God loves the person with many issues as much as he loves the person with fewer ones.

Encourage church members to care for each other as a family would. In a biological family that functions with some measure of health, the family members will celebrate victories when times are good as well as care for each other in times of hardship. Many churches are naturally good at celebrating victories and good times, such as implementing graduation parties, wedding showers, and baby showers. However, a pastor intent on leading the church as a family will also look for opportunities for the church people to gather and attend an event a church family member is participating in, such as a community play, a sporting event, or a choral production. Also, in a world where young people may not live with both parents, a high level of family care is displayed when several church people arrive to see the school performance. Such a level of caring contributes to what will make a young person stay with the church into adulthood.

Furthermore, if a biological family member becomes ill, gives birth, or enters the hospital, in a healthy family, other family members will step in to help however needed and will visit the family member in the hospital. Such a model can also manifest in a small church and is a strong indicator that the small church has truly become a family group. As the small church grows relationally and bonds as a family, this supportive behavior may spontaneously manifest as a natural outgrowth of the family connection. However, a small-church pastor can also encourage church attendees to care for each other as a family by making suggestions such as, "It would be good for a few people in our church family to take some food over to the Kayson family while Louise is in the hospital. Who is willing to volunteer to do that?"

Use the family model for activities and events. A family reunion or social gathering usually encompasses family members of all ages. The kids will sit near the adults and will visit with aunts, uncles, and cousins. There may even be an extracurricular activity planned that involves people of all ages, such as the family softball or volleyball game. Family gatherings don't usually have different activities for different age levels. Instead, the family will incorporate all ages as part of the whole event.

When a small church functions as a family, the different age groups can be merged to participate together. Many small churches don't have the staff or volunteers to support full-blown activities for each separate age group. So it's important to avoid wearing out the team with innumerable events for all different age groups. Instead, plan social events in a way that models a biological family gathering and features inclusive activities for all ages.

For instance, at one Memorial Day event at our small church, we had a churchwide cookout and included a gift table for a senior graduating from high school. While the food was being prepared, several teens and children also played catch and some folks enjoyed the horseshoes and cornhole games that were set up. After we ate, we played Heirloom Volleyball (aka Chair Volleyball) with everyone present. People aged twelve to eighty sat in folding chairs on both sides of a volleyball net and hit an oversized beach ball back and forth over the net. The fun thing about Heirloom Volleyball is that there are no rules, except that everyone must remain seated in their chairs and that the ball is dead if it goes out of bounds without a volley or hits the ground. Other than that, participants can hit the ball as many times as necessary to get it over the net. At one point, someone bounced the beach ball off my head twice in a row, and the ball was still considered live and in play.

All participants, from the youngest to the oldest, had a hilarious blast. I haven't laughed so hard since high school. After the volleyball game was over, we allowed the graduating senior to open his gifts, and he was as happy as if we had planned a fully separate event just for him. At the time of this successful event, our church averaged about thirty-five in attendance, and forty-two people attended the event. A church doesn't have to be supersized with a full-blown youth and children's program to offer ministry events for all ages and to have a roaring good time that all ages will enjoy!

Following an organization-by-age-group model, the above event would have been split into three social gatherings: a graduation party, a cookout for the adults, and a volleyball game possibly for the youth alone. Since it was planned and implemented using the family model, the whole church was involved, and it included all ages. The same family model can be used for any church activity, including merging the Easter egg hunt with the churchwide Easter luncheon. At such an event, the teens will hide the Easter eggs, the children will hunt the eggs, and the whole church will eat lunch together. After lunch, the senior adults might teach the teens how to play dominoes, the church might host a cornhole tournament, or both activities could be done. Even if a small church has only two teens and three children, it's important to work with the people who are present, to celebrate their attendance, and to provide family-based activities for all ages. As small-church leaders, it's easy to think, *We only have one teen and two children, so we don't have enough participants to even think about having youth or children's events.* The family model that welcomes people of all ages is the answer to this problem. It also allows the church to plan fewer activities, and those activities will foster a strong family bond across generational lines, thus allowing small-church leaders to pace themselves and not wear themselves out trying to plan one weekly activity after another for different age groups.

Furthermore, when there are not enough workers to have a weekly youth service/event, consider having a youth service/event once a month or once a quarter where teens in the community are invited. Having a monthly or quarterly youth service/event along with implementing the family model of including youth in churchwide events will provide a small church with a robust youth program that will result in young people fully engaging in church life. Even if the youth group is five teens or fewer, those five teens are important to the kingdom of God!

As already mentioned, the church has some organizational elements that must be implemented. However, the overarching atmosphere and theme should be rooted in a family model. The savvy pastor and lay leaders of a small church will tout the advantages of the family model as a benefit of their small church. When a visitor asks, "Do you have activities for children?" the family-model church leader can say, "Our church uses the family model for all ages. So yes, we do have activities for children, and they are included as part of our church's family focus. For instance, every fall, we have a bonfire and wiener roast where we play fun games that children and adults both enjoy, and we sit around the fire and sing songs for all ages. In a world where families are not always intact, we provide a family connection that makes all ages feel that they belong."

Small churches are not just large-church wannabes. They are spiritual family groups that the Lord uses as a fountain of his grace and goodness.

Relational Leadership Blend

Relational leadership is one of the key leadership styles of a four-part leadership model, and it is through relational leadership that a pastor can partner with lay leaders to lead a church in growing relationally. The most effective leaders view leadership styles as tools in a toolbox. A job that requires a Phillips screwdriver cannot be completed with a flathead screwdriver. The flathead screwdriver has its place and purpose and is needed, but not if the screw calls for a Phillips screwdriver. Likewise, leadership styles should be pulled out of the leadership "toolbox" and used as needed, when needed. Some jobs may call for the use of more than one tool; likewise, a leadership blend often requires the use of more than one leadership style at a time. However, the small-church pastor must be well-acquainted with the different leadership styles to know when to use them. The four best ongoing leadership styles for the small-church setting are relational leadership, collaborative leadership, transformational/spiritual leadership, and servant leadership. Relational leadership is foundational to both collaborative leadership and transformational/spiritual leadership, with servant leadership providing the condition of the heart. Please be aware that it is not the intent of this book to provide exhaustive information on each leadership style, but to provide enough information to lay a framework for the reader to implement key concepts and to pursue future reading and research.

Relational Leadership

Relational leaders have a goal of getting to know people and taking the time to build trust so that a relationship will have a strong foundation. A pastor who sets the example as a relational leader will also inspire laypeople to be relational leaders. Some specific traits of a relational leader are as follows:

- They sincerely value people for who they are, not as commodities and not for their assets.
- They focus on building healthy relationships both inside and outside the church.
- They realize healthy relationships are built on trust, and that takes time.

Relational leaders sincerely value people for who they are, not as commodities and not for their assets. A true relational leader focuses on the worth of people because they are created in the image of God. Such a leader will value the poorest person as much as the richest person. They will invest as much time in the least talented as they do the highly talented. Relational leaders don't allow the assets a person brings to the church, whether skills or gifts or money, to be the motivating factor for valuing that person. They also don't view people as commodities—something merely to be gained and counted so that the church looks good. Rather, true relational leaders concentrate on the merit of each person and have a goal of pointing others to a new relationship with Christ or a deeper relationship with Christ.

Sometimes, small churches remain small because God needs family groups to reach people who don't like large crowds and will never attend a large church.

Relational leaders focus on building healthy relationships both inside and outside the church. Relational leaders don't limit their relational skills to only people who gather inside the church, although, as already stated, church relationships are vitally important. However, relational leaders purposefully work to build relationships with people in the community, whether in their own neighborhoods, in places of employment, or through community service. Such leaders will purposefully do things such as regularly go to the same coffee shop and order from the same barista with the intention of building a relationship that ultimately leads to an invitation to church. A relational leader will find that there are plenty of opportunities outside the church walls to make an impact for Christ. When the pastor and lay leaders commit to making an impact through building relationships in the community, they will eventually see some of those people arrive at the church door. However, the goal should remain for people to know Christ or to go deeper in Christ, not to use relational leadership as a tool just to increase attendance so the church looks better.

Relational leaders realize healthy relationships are built on trust, and that takes time. One small-church pastor reports that it took a congregation about eight years to fully trust her and realize that she was not going to abandon them like a long line of short-term pastors had in the past. The church was entrenched in the foster-child syndrome, as detailed in chapter 1, and the pastor's willingness to put down roots and commit to building relationships is what finally broke through their fear of abandonment. Thus, the small-church relational mascot is a turtle because many small churches expect the pastor to leave soon anyway, and it takes time to overcome the foster-child syndrome. Furthermore, in our current culture, many people don't rush to trust leaders. Therefore, the turtle represents the slow process of earning trust and respect. Galatians 6:9 states, "Let us not become weary in doing good, for at the proper time we will reap a harvest if we do not give up." The reality is that slow growth can lead to frustration, and frustration can lead to a desire to give up on the current ministry assignment. However, Galatians 6:9 makes a promise that there is a harvest to be reaped if we will have patience and not become weary in doing what the Lord has called us to do. An acorn that sprouts into a sapling can take years to become a majestic oak tree. Likewise, a small church that has taken a few hits and perhaps survived through a long line of short-term pastors may take five to ten years to grow into a fully healthy setting. A relational pastor understands such growth is a process and that good things will come if he or she continues to persevere in building relationships.

Collaborative Leadership

When I speak at small-church conferences, after each session I always have attendees separate into small groups and discuss the concepts. Ideally, a pastor will be there with his or her church lay leaders. Together, they sit and discuss how the concepts presented pertain to their church and how they can apply those concepts to their church setting. In other words, they create a custom plan just for their church during the event.

One pastor attending such an event said, "We aren't taught to do this with our church lay leaders, and it's so eye-opening." Too many times, leadership training focuses on how pastors can ensure that churches follow *their* leadership and *their* vision. The problem with that viewpoint is that it is centered on one person and defines leadership the way *Merriam-Webster* does (one leads, another follows) and not the way Christ does (relational servanthood with a goal of empowerment and transformation). Collaborative leadership better fits Christ's definition of leadership than *Webster's* because it is not about everybody doing what one person wants to do but about that one person, in the spirit of a servant, building relationships with people and empowering them to work together for the transformation of the church. For those who think, *I need people to follow me,* Christ went so far as to say, "And do not be called leaders; for only One is your Leader, that is, Christ. But the greatest of you shall be your servant. Whoever exalts himself shall be humbled, and whoever humbles himself shall be exalted" (Matt. 23:10-12, NASB).

Therefore, when it comes to making plans for church growth and direction, the go-to leadership model should be collaborative, which is an outgrowth of relational leadership. Part of the purpose for this book is to establish a framework for a church's pastor and lay leaders to collaborate to create a tailored plan for their church. Granted, there are times when the pastor is the only one who can make a particular decision in situations such as an emergency. There are also situations that require decisions entailing confidentiality, and only the pastor and the person involved know the details. However, these situations are not meant to set the standard for day-to-day leadership in the small-church setting.

Many small churches across North America have a core group of senior adults who have held the church together for decades. This core group often has a knowledge of the church's history and of what has worked and what has not worked in that community. Friction can happen if a pastor doesn't take the time to build relationships and trust and doesn't respect the years of service the seniors have invested. I have seen situations where senior adults are even pushed aside and their voices silenced. My hope is that no one reading this book has made this mistake. However, when this disrespect happens, the senior adults will balk at any plan and won't agree to do anything. At that point, a gridlock develops, with two factions pitted against each other. The issue is not about the proposed change but about the seniors' resentment because they either fear being cast aside or are being cast aside. In many cases, the church would not exist if these seniors had not sacrificially committed their time, talents, and money through the decades. With that said, I have also seen churches with a core group of senior adults who are 100 percent invested and enthusiastic to make changes and move forward. The difference is that the pastor, practicing relational leadership and with the heart of a servant, has taken the time to build relationships and trust and to learn the history of the church. Accordingly, he or she has valued the opinions of long-standing members enough to collaborate with them in developing the plan necessary for the church's growth.

The best church leaders, whether pastors or lay leaders, inspire people to create and develop and own the plan. Therefore, collaborative leaders involve *as many people as reasonable* in the decision-making, vision and mission, and planning. People are less likely to "get in line and follow" when they have had little to no voice in the process. However, people will own what they have created. The more people have a voice and input, the more likely they are to get behind a plan.

When church leaders stop thinking, *This is what I want to do, and I want the people to follow what I want,* and start thinking, *I need to collaborate to create goals, vision, and even activities, and I need to empower the people to make our plans a reality,* there will be a change in how people respond and invest. As this book directs, it's important for church leaders to discuss the health of the church in a collaborative fashion and to give the Holy Spirit time to reveal areas of needed growth and change.

Transformational/Spiritual Leadership

In the church world, transformational leadership is knitted with spiritual leadership because the transformational goal is more than just helping people become a better version of themselves. Transformational leadership in the church focuses on the spiritual growth and improvement of congregants through the transforming power of the Holy Spirit. The pastor and lay leaders who focus on spiritual transformation in their own lives and the lives of attendees will reap the results of God's anointing, both personally and corporately. Church leaders committed to transformational leadership move away from thinking, *How can we get new people here to help increase the number of church attendees?* to thinking, *How can I invest in the lives of the people so that they experience spiritual growth, with kingdom growth flowing from it?* The transformational leader's goal is to lead others to Christ, the Great Physician and Ultimate Transformer, and to lead them into entire sanctification through the baptism with the Holy Spirit.

A transformational leader focuses on helping people know Christ, go deeper in Christ, and seek Christ for full deliverance and transformation. A pastor's staying long term at a small church to disciple attendees over time is the stuff that transformational leadership is made of.

A pastor who engages in transformational leadership will also be committed to relational leadership. Thus, he or she will be more likely to stay at a small church long term to build strong relationships and truly become part of the church family rather than be a temporary leader who is "just passing through."

Transformational leadership calls for church leaders who can see the issues, even experience some angst because of the issues, and love people so much that they will continue working with them until they find deliverance. We live in a throwaway society where people discard anything they don't like or want, including material items, relationships, and even relatives; some people discard their own children. However, it's impossible to be a transformational leader, willing to stay the course to let God do his mighty work, while expecting quick fixes that result in throwing away or neglecting human beings that Christ died for.

Sometimes, small churches are corporately steeped in issues that have plagued the church for years. Once the issues in the church are revealed, the normal human response for a pastor is to run to "a better church." However, there are no guarantees that the next church will be better; it might be worse. Frankly, it's way easier to hop from one church to the next every few years than to stay with one church and work through the corporate and private issues so that the church and the attendees can find true deliverance and transformation. Thus, the transformational pastor does not just put a Band-Aid on problems but commits to helping people overcome.

Some churches are like a garden full of big rocks (old issues) that need to be dealt with and removed. Leaders who don't practice true transformational leadership may see the rocks but pretend the rocks aren't there. In this mindset, they may even metaphorically set up some artificial plants, attach fake butterflies to the leaves, smile big, and play as if true transformation has happened. In reality, the problems have only been masked. Sometimes, this masking happens for fear of losing attendees if the deeper problems are dealt with. Sometimes, the masking occurs in the name of unity. However, unity based on ignoring issues is not unity; it's codependency. True unity is based on transparency and truth, not denial and deception. Transparency and truth are the cornerstones for authentic transformational leadership. Christ himself stated, "Then you will know the truth, and the truth will set you free" (John 8:32).

A leadership team can build an invigorating church service that spawns numerical growth where people leave church feeling good every week, but the same people can remain chained to the same issues that have plagued them for years. Transformational leaders help people move from a surface, feel-good experience to a deeper deliverance that can only be brought about through the power of the Holy Spirit. Such leaders are not interested in skimming the surface to just see bigger numbers in their church; they are interested in guiding people to put down deep roots that will lead to sustainable church growth that impacts future generations.

If you are wondering if there is any faithfulness left in a world of public moral decay, go to a small church where the devout pastor is sacrificially serving for little to no salary. There you will find faithfulness.

When a church's pastor and lay leaders commit to transformational leadership, their church will be characterized by people who find full deliverance and are ever growing in the Lord. A transformational leader focuses, not on how many people he or she can get to church so the stats look good, but on how he or she can help people who attend know Christ and go deeper in him. The deeper people go in the Lord, the more they share their faith. The more they share their faith, the more they influence others to attend church. And that's what leads to sustainable church growth.

Servant Leadership

The person who ushered in servant leadership in the latter twentieth century was Robert K. Greenleaf. His contemporary model for servant leadership was his father, a servant in the community, at work, and in the church; however, Greenleaf's ultimate model for servant leadership was Jesus Christ.[1,2] Greenleaf's book *The Servant as Leader* defines the servant leader as one who listens, serves first, possesses foresight, and persuades, rather than coerces.[3] Greenleaf challenges the reader to break away from autocratic, hierarchical leadership and adopt an attitude of service that empowers those in the leader's care.[4]

The term "servant leadership" seems to lend itself to the suggestion that the main thing a servant leader should do is serve. However, servant leadership encompasses more than just acts of service, as indicated above. I have witnessed more than one person who verbally embraced servant leadership while acting out an autocratic leadership style. True servant leaders are not autocratic leaders who serve and use servant language. I have seen some autocratic leaders who are willing to commit hours to acts of servanthood. However, anyone who joins the autocrat must serve the way the autocrat dictates, resulting in volunteers being driven away, leaving the autocrat frustrated when left to do all the work alone. Unfortunately, the autocrat may be convinced that he or she is modeling servant leadership because of his or her acts of service. Therefore, the autocrat will be so puzzled by the negative reactions of others that he or she will foist blame for the problems onto the volunteers who were repelled by the autocrat's "my way or the highway" behavior, which also flies in the face of the sanctified life.

True servant leadership is more a condition of the heart than acts of service. While acts of service are part of servant leadership, the servant leader also humbly listens before providing "all the answers," possesses a foresight that includes a God-given discernment for how his or her actions impact other people, and also uses persuasion rather than coercion.[5] The whole concept of persuasion rather than coercion is rooted in relational leadership and entails the willingness to listen to people and their concerns. When a relational servant leader takes the time to listen to people, get to know them, and build trust, those people will listen when the servant leader, in all meekness and humility, makes suggestions for needed change. I have witnessed true relational servant leaders who have used the power of persuasion, rather than coercion, to get people to cheerfully support the change they said they would never support "six months ago." I have also witnessed true autocrats, while speaking servant language, cause turmoil, division, and church splits when they use coercion to insist on changes that people simply are not ready for and insist that they, not the people, will be deciding what to change, how to change, and when to change. Such leaders also often resort to manipulation and sharing only part of the picture to get the church board to agree with them. Their mantra in such situations is "Lead, follow, or get out of the way." Unfortunately, many church attendees will get out of the way, and that will also mean leaving the church.

Robert Greenleaf was opposed to such autocratic behavior and saw how detrimental it is to those who are working with such a leader. Greenleaf was influenced by a novel, *The Journey to the East*, about a highly ranked spiritual leader, Leo, who like Christ, served first.[6] He was also influenced by the story of

Quaker John Woolman, an antislavery servant leader from the eighteenth century, who persuaded East Coast Quakers to free their slaves, one family at a time.[7,8] There were no wars, no conflicts, just a peaceful transition of slave owners releasing their slaves because Woolman peacefully persuaded them that it was the right thing to do. Such servant leaders in the church possess the wisdom and foresight to prioritize what is important in the life of the church and to listen to others as they share what they think is important. Servant leaders in the church remain committed to serving first while also giving the Holy Spirit time to work as they wait for needed changes to unfold through the efforts of their gracious persuasion.

I have seen some conflict and division in the church. I have seen some people hurt in the church. But I have seen much more harmony and unity in the church. I have seen many more people blessed and helped in the church. The church is not perfect. But I love the church. I love the relationships and fellowship in the church. I love the God who uses the church for his glory!

PAUSING TO PLAN

- Each participant should choose at least one key concept he or she found especially meaningful or applicable to

your church. As a group, discuss all the key concepts each participant has chosen.

- What are two to three ways our church is functioning well as a family?
- What are two to three ways our church can improve in functioning as a family?
- What specific ways can we implement more family language in our church?
- What are two to three things our church is doing right relationally?
- What are two to three new things our church can do to better foster relational growth?
- How are we doing in our collaborative leadership efforts so far?
- How can transformational leadership concepts be used in our church to *(a)* help people overcome deep issues and *(b)* inspire spiritual growth among the members of our congregation?
- What elements of servant leadership are we using well?
- What elements of servant leadership can we improve upon?

Five Traits of a Healthy Small Church

A healthy small church . . .
- operates as a family;
- openly welcomes new family members;
- sees spiritual growth among attendees;
- participates in the Great Commission;
- engages with the community.

"Do not despise these small beginnings, for the LORD rejoices to see the work begin"
(Zech. 4:10a, NLT).

SIX

Reaping the Growth Numerically

●————————●

But God chose the foolish things of the world to shame the wise; God chose the weak things of the world to shame the strong. God chose the lowly things of this world and the despised things—and the things that are not—to nullify the things that are, so that no one may boast before him. It is because of him that you are in Christ Jesus, who has become for us wisdom from God—that is, our righteousness, holiness and redemption. Therefore, as it is written: "Let the one who boasts boast in the Lord."

—1 Cor. 1:27-31

Afraid of the Numbers

When my son was about twelve, we were homeschooling our kids. Brett was enrolled in advanced math, which included prealgebra and studies in the twelve-based number system. He was also a sleepwalker. Bad combination.

One night, after I had gone to bed and was dozing off, I was awakened by someone shaking my shoulder.

Brett's voice penetrated my dazed mind. "Mom . . . Mom . . . !"

I opened my eyes. The hall light was on, so I could clearly see Brett's messed up curly hair, fully opened eyes, and distraught face in the shadowed room.

"Mom . . . ," he repeated as he wrung his hands.

"What's the matter, Brett?" I asked.

"Mom . . . I'm afraid of the numbers!" he urgently claimed. At this point, I knew Brett's body was with me, and even though he appeared to be wide awake, his mind was in dreamland.

"The numbers . . . they're right over there, Mom!" He pointed just past his elbow. "I'm afraid of the numbers!"

I propped myself up on my elbow so I could get closer to his face. "Brett, you're afraid of the numbers?" I asked in a doubtful voice while looking straight into his eyes.

As we held gazes, a thread of logic fluttered through his dark brown eyes, and I honestly thought he had experienced a breakthrough. However, his next words dashed all my hopes.

"I am awake! And you don't understand!" he declared in the tortured voice of a boy drowning in math overload.

The next morning, he had no memory of the episode, and now as a grown, married man, he still does not remember it.

This exchange between my son and me is quite humorous and still brings our family some chuckles. However, sometimes, small-church pastors can become "afraid of the numbers" as they contemplate the potential for low attendance as well as the necessity for statistical accounting through such measures as the annual pastor's report. They can also become perpetually disappointed with the numbers if they don't meet expectations. Neither mindset is humorous.

Disappointed with the Numbers

Early in my pastoral ministry, the Lord impressed me not to count the number of people in attendance. I remember sitting on the platform at the start of the service. I began doing what I usually did, counting the number of people in the sanctuary.

However, I received a very strong impression from on high that I should stop counting and that I should not count again. I realize all churches don't have a reliable counter, and in some settings, the pastor still needs to do the counting so that accurate church statistics can be reported. But thankfully, there was a man in our small church who was great at counting, so we relied on him to provide the required statistics. As an optimist, I immediately assumed that the Lord was stopping me from counting because the number of people was going to grow so large that I wouldn't have time to count them all.

As the years unfolded, I realized that the Lord had another lesson for me to learn—that I was not to focus on the *number* of people present; rather, I was to focus on the *people* present. I learned to appreciate and give caring attention to the people who were present rather than become frustrated by the people who were absent.

Thoughts such as *I wonder where everyone is? I'm disappointed. We expected seventy, but only fifty-five showed up* can send a silent message to attendees that they don't matter as much as absentees. Even if the thoughts are never expressed, the people present can sense the attitude and feel as if their presence isn't as important as the presence of the absentees. If the negative thoughts are expressed, the ones present may even join in the disappointment over the unmet attendance expectations, resulting in a loss of morale.

Even though I learned not to comment on the number of people not present, sometimes an attendee would express disappointment, and that's when I'd say, "I don't know where they are, but they missed a great time! The people who are here are fabulous. We had a good time! It's been a wonderful day!"

Many times, the numbers might not meet expectations. However, there will also be times when the numbers exceed expectations. That's when the temptation to take pride in the numbers can arise.

Proud of the Numbers

First Chronicles 21 recounts the story of King David's falling to the temptation to take a census of the fighting men of Israel and Judah. Verses 1-4 state,

Satan rose up against Israel and incited David to take a census of Israel. So David said to Joab and the commanders of the troops, "Go and count the Israelites from Beersheba to Dan. Then report back to me so that I may know how many there are."

But Joab replied, "May the LORD multiply his troops a hundred times over. My lord the king, are they not all my lord's subjects? Why does my lord want to do this? Why should he bring guilt on Israel?"

The king's word, however, overruled Joab; so Joab left and went throughout Israel and then came back to Jerusalem.

After David received the census results, his conscience was stricken, and he realized his count of the fighting men was not in alignment with the Lord's will. "Then David said to God, 'I have sinned greatly by doing this. Now, I beg you, take away the guilt of your servant. I have done a very foolish thing" (v. 8). David pridefully shifted his focus from the military power being in the Lord's strength to the military power being in the number of fighting men. As a result, the Lord moved against the nation of Israel, and the results were disastrous.

If pastors and lay leaders aren't careful, they can fall into David's trap of an unhealthy focus on numbers, resulting in pride if the numbers are high. However, the number of people present should never become a point of pride. "Pride goes before destruction, a haughty spirit before a fall" (Prov. 16:18). David's story is a prime example of this proverbial truth.

Numbers in Perspective

Perhaps the Lord is as disheartened with church leaders when they despair about low numbers as he is when they are proud of high numbers. This focus on numbers can marginalize the focus on the Lord and how he is working in the lives of attendees. If a church of any size shows numerical growth, the focus should remain on the work of the Lord with the souls of the people present. It should remain on the desire of the Lord to save them, entirely sanctify them, and help them to grow in his grace until he gives them a home in heaven. I believe that God wants us to be with people who are with us now, to love them, to minister to them, and to build relationships with them. Therefore, ministry attention should be on the value of the people present and the care for their eternal souls, not on the numbers.

If you focus on numbers in a small church, you will go nuts! By its very nature, the small church is, well, small. So the numbers won't be large. However, if a small church is fulfilling its mission, some new people will come and stay throughout the years. Nevertheless, that does not guarantee the actual numerical count will grow every year. There are some years when several people pass away or move. During the same year, the small church may gain new people, even new converts, but it may not gain as many people as were lost. The church technically still has had numerical growth, but the numbers won't reflect the growth.

Even though numerical growth should not be the primary focus, numerical growth can happen despite the ebb and flow of attendees moving or passing away. When the numbers are given their proper place, they could even be an indicator of positive things happening in the church. Furthermore, there are ways that a healthy small church can see numerical growth through attracting new attendees who participate in church life. The key is that churches grow spiritually, relationally, and numerically. Numerical growth without spiritual and relational growth is empty growth. Numerical growth can happen in the small church as an outflow of spiritual and relational growth. Thus, growing relationally and spiritually should be a greater focus than growing numerically, especially when we consider the people who are beginning or reigniting a relationship with the Lord.

However, the church needs to be functioning at some level of spiritual and relational health for the church to gain new attendees. Otherwise, attempts at outreach will not result in sustainable growth, and sustainable growth is the key to a small church's existence into the future. Note that churches need to be functioning at *some level* of spiritual and relational health. The intent is not to suggest that a church must be perfectly healthy both spiritually and relationally but that the church has become healthy enough to sustain growth. Most churches, like people, are works in progress, and the Lord will reveal when the church has become healthy enough to begin a sustainable outreach process. However, at any point in a church's life, the pastor and lay leaders can join with attendees to start tabulating the KING Number to encourage a focus on building the kingdom of God, which will, in turn, foster spiritual health, resulting in outreach efforts that will increase attendance.

KING Number: Kingdom Impact Numerical Growth

At the writing of this book, there is a wonderful situation occurring in a church in Palestine, Texas, that will lead to the church having a five-person loss in the next year or two. The pastor of this small church, Don Gardner, and his dear wife, Evie Gardner, served as missionaries to Africa for over thirty years. When they came back to the United States, they accepted the call to be the pastoral team at the Palestine church. Not too long after they became pastors of the small church, the Lord led a Kenyan couple to attend church with their three children. Pastor Don and Evie met the couple and immediately started speaking with them in Swahili. The Kenyan couple fell in love with the pastor, his wife, and the church and joined as full members. However, the husband, who had been enrolled in college to prepare to be an evangelist in Kenya, recently completed his degree. Within the next one to two years, the couple plans to travel back to Kenya to serve in evangelism. When that day comes, the small church will show a decrease of five in attendance and a loss in membership. Even though the church's numbers will decrease, the kingdom of God will increase as the Kenyan couple evangelizes their homeland.

This story is a good example that proves if a small church lacks numerical growth, it is not always an indicator of a lack of kingdom growth. God uses small churches to grow his kingdom in ways that can and cannot be counted. For instance, some small churches serve as a spiritual ICU where believers stop, get help, and go to the next place God has for them. "Small" is a valuable tool God can use to heal his people. However, when the Lord uses a small church in such a way, sometimes it can be overlooked, especially when the focus is placed on the church now having lower attendance because the healed person has moved on to his or her next ministry assignment. That is the reason why it is important for small-church leaders to stay focused on the impact their church is making on the kingdom of God. One of the ways to hone this focus is to calculate monthly the **Kingdom Impact Numerical Growth**—the KING Number—and then add the monthly calculations together to get the annual KING Number.

The KING Number assessment will include various ways the small church is impacting the kingdom of God. For instance, when the small church in Palestine loses the Kenyan family of five, it will add five to its KING Number because it is sending the couple to do kingdom work. The church can also count every future Kenyan convert in its KING Number because the church had a part in sending the evangelists. When a church is praying for someone to get saved in another state, and that person commits his or her life to Christ, then small-church leaders will add one to their KING Number for that month. When a church has a couple move out of town, and that couple starts a new Bible study in their neighborhood just like the one they participated in at their former church, the former church will add two to its KING Number. Then the church will continue to add to its KING Number as the fruits of the new Bible study are discerned. Any answered prayer can also be added to the KING Number. Anytime church members pray with someone who doesn't attend their church, that's a KING Number. Sending a love offering to a missionary is a KING Number; the church could add a KING Number for every dollar they give to the missionary. Tabulating the KING Number will keep small-church attendees focused on building the kingdom of God and help them recognize the true impact their small church is having for the kingdom.

In Matthew 16:18, Jesus states, "I will build my church; and the gates of hell shall not prevail against it" (KJV). One of God's goals is to build his church, his kingdom. Hence, some small churches may show no numerical growth because they are sending stations, not harbors. God may send a group from one church to establish another church, resulting in fewer attendees in the sponsoring church. He may persistently call missionaries and pastors from a church, resulting in a loss in average attendance. However, the collective ministries of those who are called may impact multitudes in God's kingdom. A lack of visible numerical growth in a small church does not always equate to a lack of kingdom impact. We fall into a trap when we focus solely on numerical growth as the measure of a church's success. God is interested in kingdom expansion.

Small churches are not small because they are failures. Rather, they successfully provide the close connection that throngs of people enjoy.

Ways to Increase Church Attendance

As already stated, a small church can see numerical growth, and there are effective ways to bring about such growth. There are programs and events that can help increase attendance that people in your church will be interested in supporting. One of the keys is tapping into your church's strengths as well as the preexisting interests of your church's attendees because people support what they're already invested in. In that context, there are three different categories of outreach efforts that small churches may want to consider:

- Organic Outreach
- Events and Activities
- Organized Community Outreach

Organic Outreach

Greg (name changed) tells the story of his work-related friendship with Patrick (name changed). Greg eventually learned that Patrick regularly attended church. However, Patrick never once invited Greg to church. What Patrick didn't know was that Greg was secretly wishing for a church invitation. Finally, Greg looked at Patrick one day and said, "Aren't you ever going to invite me to your church? I've been waiting for you to invite me for months!" At that point, Patrick extended an invitation. Greg accepted, and the rest is history. Greg has now been attending Patrick's church for decades. This true story is a haunting reminder of how there may be outreach opportunities that remain unnoticed and untapped because a church attendee doesn't recognize the power of organic outreach or his or her responsibility before God to be a willing participant with him in reaching out to others.

Organic outreach occurs when individual church attendees (not just lay leaders or pastors) reach out to people they encounter in their daily lives. Organic outreach does not involve the church group reaching out together, but church attendees individually connecting with people whom they regularly see. The idea behind organic outreach is that all regular church attendees can embrace the spiritual responsibility of caring enough for people they encounter to pray for them and take the initiative to extend an invitation to church, as the occasion arises.

Furthermore, a church business card is a wonderful tool with which to "arm" willing church attendees who want to participate in organic outreach. With bifold or trifold business cards now available, the church card could feature a photo of the church on the front with worship times and contact information inside. The business card could even include a tear-away prayer-request card.

The business card should also feature the church brand. If your small church does not have a brand, it's important for small-church pastors and leaders to work with the church body to develop a church brand—a turn of phrase that identifies your church and highlights a strength. For instance, "A small church with a big heart" has served as our church brand. Remember, the brand should be short and focused. It is different from the vision and mission statements but should be complementary to them. (For more on vision and mission, see Robert Beckett's book *Fanning the Revitalization Flame* [Bloomington, IN: WestBow, 2022].)

As Patrick and Greg's story exemplifies, organic outreach can occur in workplace connections, but it can also occur as a product of professional connections, repeated connections, neighborhood connections, and store connections, just to name a few. Organic outreach can evolve in any setting where individual church attendees regularly find themselves. For instance, if a person regularly buys lunch, it's advisable to go to the same restaurant at the same time and stand in the same line to talk to the same person. Eventually, the acquaintance can move into more of a friendship, which may lead to an invitation to church or a ministry event.

The same type of intentional connection can be fostered in a neighborhood setting. When my husband and I were pastoring our former church, I spent months purposefully building relationships with numerous people in our neighborhood as I walked near my home. In our current cultural climate, it takes time to build trust. However, as time progressed, I became friends with multiple neighbors and gradually built enough trust to begin offering to pray for them when they expressed a concern, had a loss, or experienced a problem. Eventually, the neighbors began to connect with each other, and we built a community of friends. One thing led to another, and one Saturday evening while it was pouring rain, my husband and I hosted a neighborhood cookout. We made a damp memory with twenty-one people crammed on our back porch while the rain flooded our backyard! Soon after this event, we wound up resigning from the church. However, the next pastor and wife were able to pick up where we left off, and the pastor's wife hosted a home-based Bible study that included some neighbors we knew and some we didn't know. Some of the neighbors have since visited the church.

Another way to participate in organic outreach is through grocery shopping. Whether I am a curbside pickup customer, or a grocery-store clerk is pushing out my cart to my car, I always end the encounter with reading the employee's name tag or asking, "What is your name?" Then I call the person by name and tell him or her, "I always pray for the people who load my groceries, and I'm going to pray for you today." Never once have I met with a negative response. Aside from one young man that acted as if he didn't know what to think, everyone else has been profusely grateful, including a store manager and an assistant store manager. At times, the grocery-store employee might even share a specific prayer request with me, and I usually pray for him or her in the parking lot.

The idea is for several willing church attendees from one church to commit to this type of organic outreach. Along with promises to pray for grocery-store employees, these church attendees could also hand out church business cards. Imagine the impact it would have on the lives of grocery-store employees if several people from the same church gave them church business cards with promises to pray for them. Eventually, there is a chance those grocery-store employees just might show up at church one Sunday, especially if they have also received invitations for a special event.

Events and Activities

For the sake of distinguishing church events and activities from organic outreach, it's important to note that events and activities will include the church body in an organized outreach effort that draws people to the church property. For the small-church body interested in outreach on the church grounds, events and activities are viewed as an opportunity to invite new people and not just as a time for all the regular attendees to get together to have fun or be blessed.

Church Events Based on Attendees' Interests. Instead of developing events based on what has been successful at another church, consult with your people to find out what kinds of events they can get excited about. A short trip to frustration is when a small church's pastor and lay leaders come up with an idea for a ministry event or weekly ministry that the church members have no interest in. Rather than conjecturing what might work, look to your people's hobbies and interests and creatively think about the types of events and ministries that align with those hobbies and interests. You may even want to conduct a poll to find out what their hobbies and interests are.

The following is an example of a successful church event that was based on the preexisting interests of a small congregation that averages in the fifties. This classic car show occurred at an East Texas Global Methodist church where a professional colleague of mine, Dr. Holley Collier, attends. The event is also a good example of the family model for activities, mentioned in chapter 5, because it involved attendees of all ages. The kids worked to sell food items to raise money for their children's program while the adults engaged with and managed the car show. Furthermore, church attendees and other interested parties got so enthused about the event that they donated all the food and drinks that the children sold. Along with the results Dr. Collier mentions below, the church also gained new church attendees from the event.

Dr. Collier states,

The car show was a huge success. We made roughly $650 from donations for hot dogs, chips, water, and cookies that went toward our Glory Kids program that meets Wednesday nights. We had 35-40 cars that were set up.

We had visitors galore! It was AMAZING. People stopped, and a few that I met said they live behind the church and decided to come over and visit; they had never before then been on the church property.

This [classic car show] was a success because of the commitment and investment from EVERYONE in the church. Everyone was motivated and engaged because it was a common interest of many people at church. As a result of the event, one new family decided to start attending our church. We are looking forward to next year.[1]

At last consultation, this small church was also planning to host an animal-shelter adoption day on the church grounds. Numerous people in the church are interested in animal rescue. The church is on the main thoroughfare of a small community, so the event will have high visibility in the community, just as the car show did.

Members of your congregation may not be interested in animal rescue; they may not own classic cars or have a hobby surrounding them. However, they do have interests and hobbies. Tap into those interests and hobbies to create a recurring church event or ministry that will benefit your community and your church and may result in new attendees.

Ministry Activities Based on Church's Strengths. Each church has its own set of strengths, and one church's strength may not be another church's strength. As you read about the following ideas, think about your own church's strengths and what ministry idea you can develop based on those strengths.

<u>Prayer and Fellowship Text Group.</u> One of the strengths of the first small church where my husband and I pastored was its prayer ministry. When COVID struck, we were challenged to find a way our church could stay connected, and the answer was as close as the cell phone in my hand. I sent a text to all church attendees who had cell phones and asked if they wanted to be part of our church's prayer text group; I received a strong response. I manually set up a cell phone group text so that everyone could send and receive texts from each other. Eventually, a couple agreed to manage the text group so that if someone wanted to be added or removed, they could take the lead on that responsibility. Our text group blossomed and transcended

COVID. It grew to the point that we were on the verge of creating a second prayer text group before we resigned from the church, because the limit on cell phone texts then was twenty people in a group.

The result was that the prayer text group bonded our church together in a way I never imagined. The group members shared prayer requests, but they also shared messages of encouragement and updates on their lives. For instance, when members of the text group were not at church, other members would spontaneously send a text, telling absentees they were missed. Such grassroots outreach and connection resulted in more faithful church attendance. Furthermore, it served as a big blessing to the friends and families of our text group when we told them we were immediately posting their prayer requests to the group.

There are other applications, such as the WhatsApp, that work well for the prayer-text-group concept. A Facebook prayer group is also a good idea, and people can download the Facebook app on their phones. However, this idea will not work unless everyone who wants to be part of the prayer group is on Facebook. Furthermore, we found that in our church, the text group worked so well because people were more apt to respond and engage with immediate-access texts than they would if they had to look at Facebook. Some small churches with tech-savvy attendees may develop their own app that has a place for real-time congregational messaging. Whatever way you choose to create the group, it seems that twenty to thirty is a good limit for the size of each text group. After about thirty people, the text group can get too busy. Therefore, it's perfectly acceptable for a church to have more than one prayer and fellowship text group.

Mobilizing the Senior Adults. Many small churches have a fair number of senior adults that may be retired. These senior adults bring a wealth of wisdom and skills that should be tapped into. The following two ideas are options to get your creative ideas flowing about ways you can use the strengths of the senior adults for outreach efforts on your church property.

First, consider starting a monthly Grandma Story Hour at your small church as a community outreach for children. Offer a craft that aligns with the book, and serve milk and homemade cookies because grandmas are known for milk and cookies. If possible, be prepared with two to three grandmas in different rooms for two to three reading levels. Get creative about spreading the word. Advertise the event via word of mouth, on Facebook, and at local schools, if allowed. Expect to start small and build a reputation for the place as a story time where moms and dads can take their children and rely on the content to be family friendly and the people to be trustworthy. Prepare an "About Our Church" brochure or simple flyer to hand to attendees to encourage them to visit your church's worship service.

Second, consider starting a monthly Grandpa Fix-It Day at your small church as a community outreach for anyone who wants to hone their fix-it skills. Have senior adult men take turns each month tutoring attendees about household, mechanical, or remodeling "fix-it" skills, such as simple plumbing fixes, how to install a light fixture, how to remove and install drywall, or how to change a tire and check a vehicle's filters and fluids. Serve a light snack or meal after each event. As with the Grandma Story Hour, get creative about advertising the Grandpa Fix-It Day. Hand out a church flyer or brochure to each attendee. In a world where single moms are often left to their own repairs, there is a strong chance that one of the moms who brings her children to the Grandma Story Hour may show interest in attending the Grandpa Fix-It Day.

If there are no senior adults in your church who are candidates to read to children or host a fix-it day, then find out what the senior adults in your church can do. Conduct a brainstorming session and skills inventory with your seniors to find out what their interests are, and creatively move forward from there. Too many times, senior adults are viewed as "used up" and not conducive to attracting young people to the church. However, if senior adults are mobilized to offer services from which young people will benefit, they very well can be part of a small church's effective outreach to people of all ages, including young people.

Campfire Church. One small church took its food pantry ministry to a whole new level. Instead of just handing out food to recipients and saying goodbye for the month, Pastor Rob Beckett started a Campfire Church on Sunday evenings during the autumn. The service consists of people sitting in a large circle around a campfire while they enjoy a casual time of worship that includes some guitar-led singing and a devotional. There is also a meal and s'mores, which is a must when a church gathers around a campfire. The church has made new connections with neighbors who regularly come and participate in this outdoor worship service. Pastor Rob Beckett's whole intent behind having a worship service outside is to lower barriers that neighbors might experience with the idea of entering a church building. An outdoor worship service is less intimidating for people who can now just walk over and sit around the campfire with a group of friendly neighborhood folks. Because a Campfire Church only works when the weather is not too hot or too cold, with the arrival of winter, participants transition to a Neighbor Dinner inside the church, which culminates in a group of people who were once intimidated about going inside the church now entering the church with no qualms.

During the first year of the Campfire Church's implementation, Valentine's Day occurred on Wednesday. So that Wednesday evening, Pastor Rob cooked steaks for the Neighbor Dinner, and sixty-five people attended the event in a church that averages twenty-five on Sunday mornings. Many people who attended the Valentine's Day event asked questions about the church and expressed interest in attending on Sunday mornings.[2] The Campfire Church is as simple as it is innovative, and it will attract people of all ages because children, teens, and adults enjoy the experience. Note that the campfire can be built in a fire pit if a church is within the city limits and the city prohibits open fires but allows them in fire pits.

Organized Community Outreach

Organized community outreach happens when the corporate church strategizes to impact the community as a group effort. In other words, the church people leave the church grounds to reach out to people. Organized community outreach meets people where they are and points them to the church as a safe place to find love and acceptance and a relationship with the Lord. Below is a list of suggestions for community outreach.

- Hosting a free movie in the park.
- Holding a prayer walk in a chosen neighborhood.
- Volunteering in community benevolence.
- Setting up a booth at a local festival.
- Sponsoring community benevolence.
- Sponsoring community prayer.

- Sending out mailings. Contact the chamber of commerce or post office. Some communities have a newcomer mailing in which churches are welcome to include a publicity piece.
- Using the Bless App (formerly known as Bless Every Home): https://blesseveryhome.com/index.php.
- Reaching out to public schools.

One small-church pastor shares the story about a group of senior adults in his church who wanted to do something in the community. So the pastor arranged with a local public school for the group of volunteers to hold open the school doors for students as they arrived at school every Friday morning. The principal enthusiastically agreed to the church people volunteering at her school. The volunteers embraced the task and faithfully arrived every Friday morning to hold open the school doors. They cheerfully greeted the students and made a positive impact that didn't go unnoticed. As time evolved, trust increased. Eventually, the principal recognized the faithfulness of the church volunteers and inquired if they would be willing to do more in her school. Now, they also volunteer during the school's game day on Fridays, when kids who have done well during the week are allowed to play computer games. As a result, some of the elementary and middle school students the volunteers serve are attending the church's Wednesday night kids' program.[3]

This simple outreach task illustrates that organized community outreach does not have to be complicated, costly, involve scores of people, or take up a lot of time. There are many opportunities the small church can embrace that will build goodwill between the church and the community, which will potentially result in new church attendees. Public schools alone are mission fields that often remain untapped. It's very easy to assume that no public school is open to church involvement. But the truth is that many public schools are pining for volunteers and would be thrilled to have a church begin to invest in the lives of their students. As I have spoken to small churches and engaged with their pastors and leaders, I have been blessed with the ways small churches have embraced public schools. One small church provided backpacks full of school supplies for students in need. Another small church made complimentary lunches for teachers. Yet another small church provided Christmas presents for needy students. There are enough outreach opportunities at public schools alone to keep all small churches busy until Jesus comes!

Work Smarter, Not Harder

Chances are extremely high that one small church will not be able to implement all the outreach ideas in this book. The intent of this book is not even to suggest such a goal, but rather to provide ideas that may work in your small church or that may stimulate new ideas among your church leaders. The prevailing thought behind the ideas is to work smarter, not harder. Small churches don't have an extensive paid staff; thus, church leaders must be wise about what events they plan and how the events are implemented to avoid burnout among lay leaders and the pastor. Therefore, along with a *doable* number of monthly or quarterly recurring outreach events or activities, consider creating three to four cornerstone events per year that include all ages; the events will become traditions for your church that you can build on. Also, remember that chapter 5 discusses events that use the family model that spans generations—one event that encompasses multiple activities and serves several purposes. Furthermore, it is important to pay attention to your community's culture and determine what your church may offer that is culturally specific and effective.

A couple of things that many small churches can do to work smarter, not harder, is to plan outreach for special holidays such as Easter and Christmas and advertise the option for Open Communion during these holidays. Never underestimate the power of serving Open Communion as an outreach tool. One small church gained new attendees because a Christian couple who wanted to take Communion had been refused by a church where they were not members. So they started regularly attending the small church that served Open Communion because they were equally included as Communion recipients.

Remember to take advantage of attending community events and services as well as denominational events. Instead of planning an all-church event on the church property, one small-church youth group led an all-church party at a local high school football game where their youth group members were playing ball, cheerleading, and performing in the band. After church leaders gained permission from the school, the church group enjoyed a tailgate party in the parking lot with hot dogs and chips before the game, and the event had higher attendance than their usual church activities. They took the event a step further when a youth group member suggested they prepare baggies of whole peanuts to pass out to game attendees every time their team scored a touchdown. The baggies had the church's address and contact information on them. Not only did this church activity follow the family model discussed in chapter 5, but it also served as a community outreach endeavor, and the church gained new attendees because of it. Furthermore, they all had a great time just hanging out together with very little effort going into the event.[4] Again, keep the focus on working smarter, not harder, for the purpose of kingdom expansion, not counting the numbers.

Kangaroo Church

When a small church has the right focus on kingdom expansion, and not just on an increase in numbers, the Lord will begin to move and great things will happen. Eventually, a pastor may be hosting an event that draws almost three times the Sunday morning attendance, such as the Campfire Church outside the church walls that evolved into Neighbor Dinners within the church walls. It can be exhilarating to see a small-church sanctuary filled up on Sunday morning. When a church experiences such growth, the small-church pastor and lay leaders often begin a building program. While there is nothing wrong with building programs and bigger buildings, too many times there is a big debt that goes with a new building. The big debt can eventually become a millstone around the church's neck, especially if the higher attendance and/or higher giving is not maintained for whatever reason. Then the church may begin to focus on serving the debt instead of expanding the kingdom.

Thus, there are a couple of other options to consider when numerical growth happens. First, going to two worship services on Sunday morning is always an option. This could also mean having one of the services on a different day, such as Saturday night. If a portion of your members are open to this idea, a second worship service can serve as an outreach tool.

Second, the small church could consider planting another small church within its church, which is what I call a Kangaroo Church. When a mother kangaroo births a baby, the joey crawls into the mother's pouch and stays there until it is ready to be on its own. When a small church births a church, think of the new church existing in the same building as the parent church until it is ready to branch out into its own building. Thus, the Kangaroo Church could exist for several months or years before it becomes fully independent. The advantage of a Kangaroo Church is that it costs way less to plant than a church plant that starts in a new location with overhead expenses such as rent, utilities, and insurance.

The Kangaroo Church can take multiple forms and can happen at different stages of a small church's life. The small church does not have to wait until the sanctuary is full to start a Kangaroo Church. For instance, if there is a high population of people in the area who do not speak English, a small church can take a step toward starting a Kangaroo Church by offering classes for English as a second language. The class attendees are a readily available outreach opportunity of new people weekly coming to the church. The Kangaroo Church plant could be sparked when the small church offers a meal after the class and follows up with a devotional and prayer. Even if only a few participants stay for the meal and devotional/prayer, a Kangaroo Church can eventually be planted as a microchurch. Once the microchurch grows enough to become self-sustaining, it can move to its own location. However, there is also no church law against a small church having a fully functioning second church worshipping in its building for decades.

As with any move a small church makes, a church plant must be bathed in prayer and launched only after training and time. A small church's pastor and lay leaders should only plant a church if the Lord leads and not because it's trendy and it will make the church look good. I recall a worship service when the speaker pushed for pastors to plant churches, and most of the pastors responded by going forward. However, my husband and I did not volunteer to plant a church. We were met with astonishment by those who knew we didn't follow the crowd, but we both knew that the small church we were pastoring at the time simply was not ready to plant a church. It's important to remember that the Lord will be faithful to guide when or if a church plant should be pursued.

Three "Keepers" for Small-Church Ministry:
- ### Keep it simple.
- ### Keep it focused.
- ### Keep it real.

PAUSING TO PLAN

- Each participant should choose at least one key concept he or she found especially meaningful or applicable to your church. As a group, discuss all the key concepts each participant has chosen.
- Based on the concepts found in 1 Chronicles 21:1-8, discuss how a focus on church numbers can be detrimental to ministry.
- How can we encourage church attendees to participate in organic outreach?
- What are two to three specific organic-outreach ideas we can encourage attendees to try?
- What specific ways can our church create events or programs that reflect the interests of our church's attendees and/or reflect our church's strengths?

- What are two to three events or activities our church can implement that may stimulate church growth without wearing out the team? These events could happen once, be recurring, or be annual events.
- Does our church have a method established that will acquaint us with the residents or employees in the homes or businesses surrounding our church and/or the homes of church leadership?
- Does our church consistently reach out to residents and/or employees mentioned in the question above?
- For those who answered yes to the above two questions: Is there a way our church can alter our outreach to improve it?
- For those who answered no to the above two questions: How can we begin the process of outreach in a basic, doable way without it turning into an overwhelming endeavor?
- What are two to three community outreach efforts our church can implement or participate in that may stimulate church growth?
- Is our church ready to plant a Kangaroo Church?
- Is there an opportunity in our community (e.g., offering classes for English as a second language) that we are overlooking that could lead to a Kangaroo Church plant?

Ten Traits of a Good Small-Church Lay Leader

A good small-church lay leader . . .

- faithfully attends all church services unless there is an unavoidable hindrance;
- diligently prays for his or her pastor and church;
- makes certain the pastoral family is financially cared for to the best of the church's ability, including gifts for birthdays, wedding anniversaries, and holidays;
- serves as a reliable volunteer;
- never says, "It's the pastor's job to do everything, since he/she gets paid";
- visits church attendees in the hospital without being asked to do so just because he or she loves members of the church family;
- faithfully tithes and even sacrificially gives as needed;
- lives a Spirit-filled life and manifests the fruit of the Spirit (Gal. 5:22-23);
- does not contribute to church conflict;
- participates in community outreach and evangelism.

"We always thank God, the Father of our Lord Jesus Christ, when we pray for you, because we have heard of your faith in Christ Jesus and of the love you have for all God's people" (Col. 1:3-4).

SEVEN

Reviewing the Challenges
Last-Stop Café, Volunteers, Burnout, and Money

●————————————●

But we have this treasure in jars of clay to show that this all-surpassing power is from God and not from us. We are hard pressed on every side, but not crushed; perplexed, but not in despair; persecuted, but not abandoned; struck down, but not destroyed.

—2 Cor. 4:7-9

Challenge No. 1: Last-Stop Café

Last-Stop Café sits as the last business on a road that stretches from downtown into the foggy unknown. Up the street from Last-Stop Café is Feel-Good Buffet, and people drive by it to get to Last-Stop Café. Many people who enter Last-Stop Café are in a life crisis, and they come into the café looking for a place to find support and guidance. The café managers develop a relationship with the newcomers and invest in their lives as they acquaint them with the Bread of Life.

Eventually, the newcomers will have a meeting with the café's owner—a man in his early thirties with nail scars in his hands. The man will sit down with the newcomers and tell them everything they have ever done. He will then explain that he can help them overcome their crises and that their lives can be turned around. All they must do is repent of their sins and agree to allow him to remove the chains of bondage. At this point, some newcomers will embrace the café owner, allow him to break their chains, consecrate their lives to the Lord, and live lives of holiness. However, other newcomers realize that the café owner is asking them to give up some of the chains of bondage they enjoy and that he also wants them to walk a straight and narrow path that leads to righteousness.

Resistant newcomers will gaze back up the street to Feel-Good Buffet and decide to go visit that establishment in the hope of feeling better about themselves and their problems. When newcomers walk into Feel-Good Buffet, the atmosphere seems joyous and light, and everyone is having a great time. The buffet features all kinds of choices, and newcomers are free to choose any desired combination, even if some of it doesn't make logical sense. There is nothing that fully resembles the Bread of Life at Last-Stop Café, but newcomers decide that's fine. After all, as long as people feel good, that's all that matters. Right? And at Feel-Good Buffet, everybody who enters is applauded. Ironically, Feel-Good Buffet has a large picture hanging on the wall of some man who looks just like the café owner from down the street. But that guy never once shows up to talk about repentance, release from bondage, or a straight and narrow path of righteousness. After a good season of eating from the buffet and feeling better all the time, newcomers begin to think it's time to continue with life as it always has been.

That's when newcomers will get into their cars and drive past Last-Stop Café, ignoring the managers and owner, who are waving for them to stop. Instead, newcomers have fully embraced Feel-Good Buffet's theology that it's OK to keep on doing life as they have always done it, and they drive straight into the fog, fully expecting to continue as usual with no ramifications because, after all, there's grace. But the blinding fog hinders their vision to the point that they cannot see the cliff before it's too late, and they drive their vehicles into a crashing demise.

When a small church serves as Last-Stop Café, it can be an honor and a challenge. Knowing that the Lord trusts a small church's pastor and lay leaders to be the beacon of truth to a person who needs full deliverance before it's too late is a high honor. If the Lord is leading people to a church, and those people desperately need to hear they must repent and break away from bondage, then the Lord knows that church will state the truth: being a Christian is not just a feel-good experience with no spiritual accountability. This means that the Holy Spirit is fully at work in that church and that conviction will occur when a person needs to turn from his or her sins. It means that Jesus Christ will do what he did in the New Testament: he will encounter newcomers and bring them to a crossroads where they must choose between the straight and narrow pathway of righteousness or the broad and easy pathway of least resistance. Thankfully, some people do choose the straight and narrow path and find deliverance.

The challenge happens when newcomers don't listen and, instead, go to the church up the street that makes them feel good, with no conviction and no call to repentance. From there, the managers of Last-Stop Café can be tempted to be discouraged because kindly speaking the truth in love, at times, leads to losing attendees when people don't want to hear the truth.

In this anti-truth mindset, they want to be affirmed in their sins because it can hurt to give up some beloved bondage. The tragedy is that too often they don't stay at Feel-Good Buffet any longer than they stayed at Last-Stop Café; they only stay long enough to feel confident in doing life their way until they drive into the fog and off the cliff.

When I speak at small-church events, I often jokingly say that sometimes Jesus is not the best church-growth partner. The truth is that Jesus is interested more in the destiny of a person's eternal soul than in whether a church's attendance numbers look good. As the New Testament reveals, not everyone believed on Christ as the Son of God, and some people even crucified him. A person's encounter with Christ doesn't always lead to repentance. Sometimes, it leads to rejection of the true Spirit of Christ.

You will not lead people to the Lord by affirming or participating in their sin.

After a few years in pastoral ministry, I started calling our small church Last-Stop Café because there were people who passed through who said no to Jesus and then drove off into the fog to their spiritual or physical demise, and no amount of love, compassion, or understanding could stop them. Their commitment to their bondage was greater than their desire to fully experience God. However, I decided early on that I'd rather be the pastor at Last-Stop Café than Feel-Good Buffet because when I face the Lord in eternity, I want him to say, "Well done, my good and faithful servant," not "Why did you sacrifice truth on the altar of appeasing consumers for church expansion?"

Challenge No. 2: Volunteers

The consumer culture not only leads to "Feel-Good Buffet" churches that focus on appeasing consumers but also results in volunteer issues. As mentioned in chapter 1, when people attend church for what they can get, they have no thought for what they can give. If small-church pastors and lay leaders are not made aware that the declining interest in volunteering is a problem that spans many churches, it would be very easy for them to think the problem is limited to just their churches or communities. However, the issue is a much larger cultural problem that also manifests itself in Europe and impacts nonprofit organizations, not just churches.[1,2] Clearly, the main reason people participate in religious organizations is linked to their religiosity and belief in God; however, the younger generation is evidencing a less fervent attachment to religious institutions and, therefore, a declining inclination to attend and volunteer, leading to an aging volunteer base.[3,4,5] Since small churches are at the bottom of the consumer chain, they are likely to feel the weight of this decline in attendance because most small churches do not have paid staff to replace the missing volunteer base.[6,7]

In this context, it is easy for small-church pastors and lay leaders to give in to the consumer urge to compete with other churches and, thus, become the driving force behind multiple programs for which church people have little to no interest in supporting as participants or volunteers. Unfortunately, sustainable church growth will not occur when a pastor and one or two lay leaders are doing most, if not all, of the church work. Therefore, pastors and lay leaders should work together to determine what *high-quality* ministries the church can offer that will have the support of attendees and will be meaningful for outreach. High-quality ministries will happen when the people involved have the time to invest in the ministry, and that cannot happen when the goal is for quantity, or the "highest number of ministries our church can possibly offer," which will quickly evolve into not having the volunteer base needed to support all the ministries.

Another challenge that evolves with volunteers is that people who volunteer are not motivated by the same principles as paid staff.[8,9] When paid staff members believe their jobs and livelihoods are at risk, the ones that are wise will not be disrespectful to their bosses and will not randomly skip work with no explanation. However, if a volunteer acts disrespectful to church leadership, doesn't show up, or quits, there is no threat to his or her livelihood. If a volunteer quits, he or she will even gain more time in his or her schedule. Furthermore, some small-church pastors and lay leaders have found themselves under attack from unhappy or dysfunctional volunteers who would never attack their bosses at work. Thus, small-church pastors and lay leaders should not use the same methods of volunteer management as they do for employee management.

With that said, volunteers can be motivated to stay committed to their duties long term, but there are some key factors that help to ensure their commitment. The first key factor involves volunteers responding well to a decentralized, caring management style that incorporates praise and support.[10,11] While an autocratic leadership approach that commands volunteers to follow orders will most likely drive away volunteers, a decentralized leadership style that incorporates servant, relational, transformational, and collaborative leadership is more likely to encourage a longer commitment from volunteers. Also, when the pastor, lay leaders, and even fellow volunteers show as much appreciation as possible for volunteers, it is a great morale booster and a wonderful way to make them feel that what they are doing is worthwhile and should be continued.[12,13]

A second key factor that ensures volunteer commitment involves a church providing volunteers with as much training and mentoring as possible. Such training makes them feel empowered and capable, rather than inadequate and overwhelmed, as they grapple to fill a position for which they are not adequately trained.[14,15,16] Whether training happens internally, as part of a denominational lay-training certification, or through both, all training is of value and will give the volunteer a foundation for confidence while fulfilling their duties. Furthermore, earned certifications can provide a motive for volunteers to serve because they gain something of value from the experience.

Third, prospective volunteers are more likely to agree to serve when they are assured that they won't be trapped in ministry positions with no breaks "until Jesus comes." Thus, it is important for small-church pastors and lay leaders to build breaks into the schedule. For instance, some ministries lend themselves to a seasonal break, such as taking the summer off or taking December off. Also, most ministries can be organized with coleaders or backup volunteers who will fill positions when needed.

Developing coleaders or backup volunteers may seem unattainable for a small church that averages fewer than fifty attendees. However, when a small church commits to only high-quality ministries that it has the resources to reasonably support, then there will be fewer ministries, with higher sustainability for each ministry. If a small church cannot sustain a long list of ministries, then it is wiser to focus on investing in fewer ministries that can be sustained into the future. In this context, there will be more people available to invest in the ministries that are offered. In other words, all possible volunteers won't have to spread their energies across numerous church ministries. More than one volunteer can then be assigned to a ministry leadership position.

For instance, one small church that averages in the twenties and thirties has one adult Sunday school class for all ages. Sometimes, even teenagers attend the class. The class has one main teacher. However, there are three other people who also teach the class when the lead teacher is out of town or needs a break. Note that all three of the backup teachers are also involved in at least one other church ministry. However, they are willing to serve as backup teachers because they are not asked to teach often, since there are three of them. Some jobs, such as greeters, allow for a rotation of volunteers so that each member of a team of four greeters would only have to serve as greeter one Sunday a month. When volunteers have breaks, it leads to greater longevity of service and reduces the chances that they will experience burnout, which can be a problem among long-standing volunteers; but more often, burnout manifests itself in pastors who are overburdened and underrested.

Challenge No. 3: Burnout

The Connection to the Consumer Culture and Volunteers

As mentioned in this book's preface, my *Pastoral Psychology* journal article demonstrates a link between small-church clergy burnout and a lack of training in the consumer culture and managing volunteers.[17] When small-church clergy are not trained to understand the consumer culture's impact on their churches, they may fall prey to working harder and harder to retain consumer attendees, while some church volunteers do less and less because they, too, are approaching the church as consumers. Because the consumer culture is a force that propels this behavior, the cycle of a pastor overworking to compensate can be never-ending. In this context, physical exhaustion sets in, followed by emotional exhaustion, and, finally, spiritual exhaustion, culminating in burnout. One study even indicates that small-church clergy may have a higher propensity to burnout than large-church clergy.[18] Since most small churches don't have paid staff, the small-church pastor can find himself or herself doing the duties of several volunteers as he or she also performs pastoral duties. Therefore, it is imperative for small-church pastors to understand not only the impact of the consumer culture but also the best ways to engage with volunteers so they will be more likely to stay committed to their posts.

Many small-church pastors are not told enough how important they are and how much of a lasting impact they are making on the hearts and lives of those to whom they minister.

The Connection to Servant Leadership

Another issue that may fuel burnout is when servant leadership meets the consumer culture. If a pastor or lay leader is serving overtime "because that's what servant leaders do," and many attendees are in a consumer mindset, then an unhealthy dynamic can unfold. When one or two or just a few church leaders serve a never-ending consumer demand without healthy boundaries, they may finally drop from exhaustion, which contributes to burnout. As indicated in chapter 5, servant leadership is a condition of the heart that should entail not only serving but also foresight, humbly listening, and using persuasion rather than coercion. Thus, when healthy servant leadership is implemented, it will be a multifaceted leadership style that includes boundaries on the time committed to acts of service. Overserving a never-ending consumer demand with no boundaries lends itself more to slavery than true servant leadership. While it is important for committed lay leaders to be aware of burnout and not fall prey to it, burnout in the church is more often manifested by the pastor. Therefore, it is imperative that pastors be on the defensive against burnout. Pastors should guard the spiritual, emotional, and physical health of themselves and their families. Otherwise, burnout will creep in and families will be sacrificed on the altar of too many acts of service.

Given this dynamic, it's a good thing for pastors to keep a monthly log of everything they do as pastors and turn that log in at each board meeting. Such a log will give board members a clear picture of the overload most small-church pastors are under, which is multiplied greatly if they are bivocational. The log will also help the pastor and board members avoid starting more programs without strong congregational support so that the pastor becomes even more overloaded.

"Our small church has more money
than we know what to do with!"
said no small-church pastor ever.

Challenge No. 4: Money

Bivocational Ministry

Part of the evidence of the consumer culture's impact on small-church pastors is that so many pastors now serve as bivocational ministers, working a part-time or full-time job to make ends meet. In a perfect world with no consumer influence, the small-church pastor could focus solely on ministry and have no worries about his or her livelihood. However, we don't live in a perfect world, and the consumer culture has taken its toll on church income. As mentioned in chapter 1, consumer attendees may not consistently tithe because they want to have greater purchasing power, resulting in less money in the church treasury. Less money means a lower ability to provide for the pastor. If you are a bivocational pastor, perhaps with a spouse who also works outside the church, know that the concept is as old as the New Testament. The apostle Paul served as a bivocational minister, as indicated in Acts 18:1-4: "After this, Paul left Athens and went to Corinth. There he met a Jew named Aquila . . . with his wife Priscilla. . . . Paul went to see them, and because he was a tentmaker as they were, he stayed and worked with them. Every sabbath he reasoned in the synagogue, trying to persuade Jews and Greeks." Paul, the biggest contributor to the New Testament, had to roll up his sleeves and work to support himself in ministry. Therefore, there should be no shame in a small-church pastor doing the same thing.

While being a bivocational pastor does have its challenges, it can also have benefits. A bivocational ministry model provides better financial stability for the pastoral family. It also creates a sacrificial model that inspires hardworking laypeople to partner with the pastor in serving in the church. Bivocational ministry additionally gives pastors outreach opportunities to coworkers. Furthermore, bivocational pastors may be more likely to put down roots in the community and stay long term at a church. When the church fit is good, a pastor's long-term commitment to the church will benefit his or her family's stability as well as the church's stability. As mentioned in chapter 1, if the foster-child syndrome is an issue, a pastor's long-term commitment will provide a remedy.

Even though there are advantages to bivocational ministry, there are also significant disadvantages. If a pastor is bivocational, that means there will be less time for hands-on ministry, meaning that some of the tasks pastors complete behind the scenes may need to be completed by committed laypeople. Not only can ministry time be minimized, but also family time can be minimized, resulting in stress on the pastor's marriage and a reduced investment in the lives of any children at home. As already mentioned, when a pastor is filling a full-time obligation to a church plus a part-time or full-time obligation to a second job, there is a greater threat of physical exhaustion, which can be a contributing factor to burnout.

When it is necessary for a pastor to be bivocational, it is equally necessary for the pastor and church lay leaders to develop some foundational strategies that fit the bivocational pastoral model. If the small-church pastor is working another job and the church people are still functioning as if the pastor's only job is at the church, then the pastor may quickly become overburdened and lose heart. One person cannot consistently do the work of several people and remain unaffected, no matter how spiritual that person may be. Thus, as already indicated, the wise pastor will be transparent with lay leaders about what duties he or she has fulfilled, including the hours at the second job and the duties at the church.

Also, lay leaders need to partner with the pastor in shifting church attendees out of thinking, *The pastor only works one job at the church*, to thinking, *The pastor is working two jobs, and we need to work with him/her in a team ministry*. Team ministry may sound like a high-maintenance, lofty goal, but the concept is quite simple and doable. Lay leaders who are joining with the pastor in team ministry will listen for opportunities to say, "I've got this one, Pastor." "This one" may include a hospital visit during the day when the pastor is working, a couple of laypeople who commit to taking care of the churchyard, three people who take charge of cleaning the church, or any number of tasks that a full-time small-church pastor may complete as part of the week's work. However, the team ministry concept only works if the pastor will accept the help. When a church is functioning in team ministry, a pastor should never say, "No. That's OK. I've got it," because when a bivocational pastor declines assistance, it works against a healthy pace in ministry.

If a small-church pastor is going to function in the bivocational model long term, then he or she must set realistic boundaries for pacing. As bivocational, small-church copastors, my husband and I have made a commitment that we will not compromise time with our family or our marriage and that we will pace ourselves. Because of this strong commitment, we function within a set of boundaries that protect us from over-extending. While establishing boundaries may sound formal, sometimes it is as simple as an informal conversation that leads to an agreement of spoken expectations that are firmly adhered to. For instance, when one of us sees the other one is doing too much, we will speak up with a warning that we pledge to heed.

When our kids were at home, we also committed to spending quality time with them, which included listening to them and attending all their extracurricular activities and special events. There was a time or two that the church was having an event, and one of us was not present because we had promised our kids to be there for them. Not only did we make our commitment known to our church lay leaders, but we also encouraged them to follow our model in placing their families first. We are both thankful that our children never rebelled as teenagers, and we have continued to cultivate a healthy relationship with them in their adulthood. Furthermore, they are also loyal church members who give of their time and resources to further the kingdom of God. There should be no expectation or reason for a pastor to sacrifice his or her family to serve a church.

When bivocational ministry is approached with balance, it can be a blessing and the challenges can be effectively managed. One way to bring balance to the bivocational model is for a small-church pastor to choose employment that is flexible, if possible, so that he or she can determine the maximum number of hours for church work and the second job. Another way to bring balance to the bivocational model is for pastors to take regularly scheduled breaks from ministry. Any pastor should be willing to take breaks from ministry, including sabbaticals and vacations, but such breaks can be a lifeline to a bivocational pastor. Serving at two jobs year in and year out with few to no breaks is beyond burnout. It's a short trip to the cemetery. So it is good for bivocational pastors to take a full vacation of at least two weeks once a year, a weekend off at least once a year, and a two-to-three-month sabbatical at least every four years. The standard recommendation between sabbaticals is often five to seven years. While four years might seem like a short stretch between sabbaticals, when we consider that the bivocational pastor is working two jobs, it isn't that short a time span at all, and during especially stressful seasons, a sabbatical every three years might be a wise consideration. Remember, the goal is for long-term, sustainable pastoral ministry, and a pastor taking time to invest in rest and self-care is the stuff that long-term, sustainable ministry is made of. Psalm 27:14 states, "Wait for the Lord; be strong and take heart and wait for the Lord," and planned breaks in ministry give pastors time to do exactly that.

Small-Church Finances

The small-church pastor's financial challenges are fueled by the small church's financial challenges. Granted, there are some small churches who have significant money in the bank, but as the twenty-first century continues to unfold, such scenarios are not the norm. Often, a small church is faced with the challenge of being on a tight budget. In some cases, this challenge can seem insurmountable and counterproductive to ministry, leading to discouragement and feelings of defeat. However, the following suggestions represent some financial strategies that contribute to the financial stability of the small church.

- *Teach about the consumer culture.* As indicated in chapter 1, it is important for pastors to teach attendees about the impact of the consumer culture. If the consumer culture's influence is fueling church attendees' lack of consistent giving, teaching about the consumer culture will help them recognize its effects, repent, and place tithing as a priority in their lives.

- *Hold a stewardship month.* January is a good month to have a stewardship emphasis that underscores the importance of church attendees supporting the kingdom of God with their time, talents, and money.

- *Schedule a periodic financial overview.* Create and print a simple financial overview that an average person can understand, and give it to attendees on a regular basis, at least every other month. It should contain the total church income, a list of the expenses by category, and the treasury balance. Keeping the financial categories broad and simple will allow the document to be condensed to half a page. If your small church has a bulletin, insert the document in the bulletin. When attendees are aware of the church's financial need, they are often more motivated to contribute.

- *Tithe on Tithe (TNT) for allocations.* When a small church has denominational obligations to pay allocations to support missions and district endeavors, it is easy to neglect paying these allocations in preference for using money for local needs. However, a church's investment in missions and being a team player for denominational support is vitally important. Therefore, a good way to stimulate giving for allocations is to implement a Tithe on Tithe (TNT) strategy. To calculate TNT, simply multiply the amount of tithe by 10 percent and add this amount to the tithe. For instance, a person paying $100 in tithe would multiply $100 times 10 percent and get a total of $10. Therefore, the final donation amount would be $110, with $10 designated as TNT for allocations. Many faithful givers are willing to give an extra 10 percent of their tithes, and TNT provides a wonderful boost to church finances that helps cover allocations.

- *Avoid the "one large giver" trap.* Most small-church pastors and lay leaders would love to have the "problem" of one donor who gives a large sum of money every month. While having a church attendee who can provide a significant monthly contribution is a good thing, it can also lead to making financial decisions based on that one person's contributions. Such a scenario can be a financial train wreck ready to happen if the major donor moves or passes away. Therefore, if a small church has one large giver, it's best to avoid practices such as going into debt with the expectation that the large donor's contributions will be the major means of paying the debt.

- *Stay out of debt.* It's best to stay out of debt, if possible. A small church may experience a season of growth with expectations and emotions high, and church leaders may begin to think that going into debt is a good solution for what seems to be an imminent need. However, numerical church growth can have its ebb and flow. As indicated in chapter 6, a big debt can become a major future obstacle if the level of financial income isn't sustained. While we live in an age where reasonable debt may be inevitable for buildings and parsonages, any decisions for debt should be prayerfully made and not based on excitement or emotional highs. A savvy small-church pastor will look beyond his or her tenure at the church to what is best for the church in the distant future.

- *Avoid out-of-balance benevolence.* One small-church pastor was noted for having a generous heart and never turning down anyone who was in need. While that may sound commendable, he put the church in serious financial peril. Word spread through the impoverished, drug-ridden community that this pastor would give money to anyone who asked. Eventually, there was a recurring long line of people in the church foyer with their hands out for money. The pastor freely gave to them from the church's coffers with no system set up to vet whether the needs were legitimate, resulting in the church's financial anemia. Most churches will encounter people who ask for help with their electric bill, groceries, or the needs of their children. Unfortunately, some of the stories used to wrench the heart are not true and are used to fuel irresponsibility, addiction, or unnecessary dependency. It is, thus, vitally important to listen to the Holy Spirit when determining who and when to help.

    If the church is not large enough to establish a balanced community benevolence that deals with the root causes of poverty, then it's always acceptable for a church to make a monthly donation to a trustworthy community service that does so and then direct people to that service. Another good idea is to print out a list of community services for people asking for help and give them that list, even if the people are also receiving assistance from your church. Furthermore, any church-supported community service endeavor, such as a food pantry, should also include an interest in people's souls and sharing the love of Christ. While the New Testament absolutely instructs us to feed the hungry and care for the needy, Christ died to save souls. As already mentioned in chapter 4, when we participate with the Lord in sharing the plan of salvation, we align ourselves and our church with the heart of God.

When a person faces many challenges in ministry, that is no indication the person is out of God's will. In Matthew 14:22-33, the disciples sailed straight into high winds and waves simply because they obeyed Christ.

PAUSING TO PLAN

- Each participant should choose at least one key concept he or she found especially meaningful or applicable to your church. As a group, discuss all the key concepts each participant has chosen.
- Discuss Last-Stop Café and determine if the Lord is using your church as a Last-Stop Café. If so, discuss how to recognize people who the Lord is bringing to your "Last-Stop Café" church and develop a prayer strategy for them to make the right decision for Christ.
- Answer the following question: How can we apply the information about volunteers to develop a stronger volunteer base for our church?
- Honestly evaluate the number of your church's ministries and answer the following question: Do we have a reasonable number of ministries for our volunteer base to sustain?

- If the answer to the above question is no, then prayerfully strategize to determine what high-quality ministries your church can sustain.
- After evaluating the pastor's documentation of duties performed over the last month, determine if the pastor's schedule is conducive to burnout. If the answer is yes, answer the following question: How can our church lay leaders help our pastor not be overburdened and under-rested?
- Discuss the financial strategies listed at the close of this chapter. Determine which ones would be beneficial for your church to implement, and then develop a plan to implement them.

Top 10 Roles of a Small-Church Pastor

10. Chief Exterminator: Insects, squirrels, lizards, snakes, rats, bats.

9. Lead Plumber and Janitor: Have plunger—will plunge!

8. Churchyard Care Provider: But only if the church mower will crank.

7. Undercover Private Eye: And now they're stealing toilet paper. Really!?

6. Animal Patrol: Because they keep dropping off strays in the churchyard.

5. Contractor: For the new church building. Lord, help me!

4. Psychologist: I'm here to counsel and help (even though *I* may need counseling after this session).

3. Loving Pastor: Who holds that baby and never reacts when the diaper leaks all over the new suit.

2. Prayer Warrior: "Dear Lord, please keep that mouse away from the front of the church during the family-altar prayer time."

1. Preacher: Who has no need to create a sermon illustration for the Exodus plagues. The insect invasion was sufficient.

"I have become all things to all people so that by all possible means I might save some" (1 Cor. 9:22b).

EIGHT

Reviewing the Challenges
BATS

●────────●

*When Jesus looked up and saw a great crowd coming toward him, he
said to Philip, "Where shall we buy bread for these people to eat?" He
asked this only to test him, for he already had in mind what he was going
to do.*

*Philip answered him, "It would take more than half a year's wages to
buy enough bread for each one to have a bite!"*

*Another of his disciples, Andrew, Simon Peter's brother, spoke up,
"Here is a boy with five small barley loaves and two small fish, but how
far will they go among so many?"*

—John 6:5-9

BATS!

One Sunday night, a pastor locked up the church after a
good evening service. Everything was fine with the sanctuary,
as usual, and the pastor expected it to be the same the next
time he opened the door. However, his expectations were soon
dashed to bits.

The next time the pastor opened the sanctuary door, he
was faced with an invasion of bats. Bats were everywhere, all

over the sanctuary, hanging from the crown molding, doing what bats do—dropping piles of feces on the carpeted floor.

Soon, the pastor had enlisted a group of trusted lay leaders, and they began to attack the bats in the most logical way they could determine—with tennis rackets. As the bats would swoop down, the church leaders would hit them like tennis balls and kill them with tennis rackets. Despite the initial vision of the plan working, it was not as effective as they had hoped, so they consulted with a game warden.

The game warden told them that the bats were a protected species and that the tennis-racket extermination campaign must immediately cease. That's when they shifted to fishing nets and pillowcases. They captured the bats with the fishing nets, dumped them in the pillowcases, and set them free. Fortunately, the church leaders also found the entry hole where the bats were invading the building and closed it so that no new invasions could occur.

Even though all churches may not experience a literal bat invasion, some small churches may have an infestation of metaphoric BATS that they don't even recognize (and I'm not talking about difficult people). Indeed, one of the biggest pitfalls a small church can fall into is the BATS pit.

Actually, BATS are in the Bible. There is a place in Scripture where the disciples had BATS. The well-known story unfolds in John 6:1-14 when Jesus feeds the hungry multitude of five thousand men (plus women and children who may have also been present). Jesus worked a miracle with a faithful boy's simple offering of five barley loaves and two fish. However, the disciples showed no signs of believing that Jesus could miraculously deal with the hunger problem or that the boy's offering would in any way feed the massive crowd, because their hearts and minds were plagued with BATS:

- **Belief Deficit**
- **Attitudes Gone Wrong**
- **Talking Negative**
- **Sins Unseen**

Belief Deficit

The disciples didn't even consider that Jesus could multiply the loaves and fish. There is no indication in Scripture that any of the disciples solicited the little boy's help with the much-needed meal. None of them said, "Hey, little guy! We see you have five barley loaves and a couple of fish. Wow! We believe with all our hearts that Jesus can do amazing things with your loaves and fish, and he can multiply them to feed these masses of people."

No! Instead, we see a case of Belief Deficit when Andrew says, "Here is a boy with five *small* barley loaves and two *small* fish, but how far will they go among so many?" (John 6:9; emphasis added). Since Andrew shows no sign of believing the little boy's offering could feed the crowd, it's logical to speculate that perhaps the little boy approached Andrew with a tug on his tunic and a faith-filled offer: "Mr. Disciple! Mr. Disciple! I have five loaves and two fish that Jesus can have to feed these people."

I am reminded of the time twenty-five years ago when our son, who was about five, offered all the money he had to help with the cost of a family vacation we were wondering if we could afford, and all he had was fifty cents. My son had faith that his offering would make a big impact on our final decision. Likewise, there is a possibility that the little boy, in childlike trust, did not model the disciples in their Belief Deficit. Instead, he may have manifested Belief Overload. If so, Jesus honored his belief.

Unfortunately, sometimes small churches can get trapped in the pitfall of Belief Deficit. Like the disciples, they can start thinking, *All we have is a* small *church with a* small *congregation. What can Jesus do with us? We're as insignificant as a handful of sand on a massive beach.* However, that is the first thing Satan wants small-church leaders to think, and the last thing God wants them to think. When small-church leaders view the gifts they have to offer to Christ as insignificant, it's a clear sign that Belief Deficit will cause Attitudes Gone Wrong.

Attitudes Gone Wrong

Not only did the disciples manifest Belief Deficit, but Andrew was also immersed in Attitudes Gone Wrong. We know his attitude wasn't right because of the way he spoke of the little boy. In so many words, Andrew said, "He's insignificant, and what he has is insignificant." His attitude toward the little boy was that he was irrelevant, too small, and his offering to Jesus wasn't even worth consideration.

When small-church leaders adopt Attitudes Gone Wrong about their church, they are digging themselves deeper into a pit of church stagnation. The wilderness journey of the children of Israel can become a church's journey. Like the children of Israel, a small church can find deliverance from the bondage of "Egypt" but not step into God's "promised land" because of thanklessness, complaining, and grumbling. In other words, churches can get spiritually stuck in the wilderness because of bad attitudes about the significance of their church.

Along with Andrew, Philip also demonstrated a lack of understanding that Christ's power was bigger than the crowd's hunger. As Philip and Andrew both demonstrate, if we allow Belief Deficit to cause Attitudes Gone Wrong, that leads to Talking Negative. The last thing that needs to happen in this cultural climate is for church leaders to embrace the consumer mindset that their church really isn't significant and then start Talking Negative.

Talking Negative

Andrew didn't hesitate to share his thoughts, and his thoughts were negative. Thus, his words were negative. His words represented the reality of Jesus's powers and abilities about as much as a wadded-up, soggy hamburger wrapper is the image of the hamburger it once contained. Proverbs 18:21 states that "death and life are in the power of the tongue" (KJV), and Andrew spoke death over that little boy's offering.

Andrew fell into the pit small-church leaders can fall into. He started Talking Negative. The mantra goes like this: "This church is so small that it's not going to ever do anything. There is no way we can 'compete' in a world where large churches seem to attract all consumers. We might as well just close the church and put us all out of our misery." Talking Negative makes no room for the power of Christ at work in the lives of the throngs of believers who attend small churches. When we talk negative about our small churches, we say to the Lord what Philip and Andrew said: "We have no faith that God can do something great."

Unfortunately, Belief Deficit, Attitudes Gone Wrong, and Talking Negative can creep into the lives of small-church leaders, and they don't even realize they're living among an infestation of invisible BATS, known as the Sins Unseen syndrome.

Sins Unseen

As mentioned in chapter 3, Psalm 19:12-13 states, "But who can discern their own errors? Forgive my hidden faults. Keep your servant also from willful sins; may they not rule over me." This passage of Scripture speaks of two types of sin: willful, known sin and hidden faults/sins. Two lines from a Robert Burns poem go like this: "To see ourselves as others see us! / It would from many a blunder free us."[1] The truth is, most people, even consecrated believers, can have blind spots—areas of their lives where they cannot see a fault or sin that others can clearly see. The disciples had a BAT infestation, and they had no clue they were so batty. They very likely thought they were just being honest and realistic about a hopeless situation—a bunch of hungry people and not enough food to go around. As Philip realistically indicated, "It would take more than half a year's wages to buy enough bread for each one to have a bite!" (John 6:7).

Like the disciples, small-church pastors and lay leaders can view their lack of belief, defeated attitudes, and negative talk about the church as simply being realistic and stating the truth. What small-church leaders need to determine is what the truth is according to Christ. The truth according to Christ about the little boy's loaves and fish is that Christ had the power to work a miracle and multiply the little boy's offering beyond the realm of the disciples' BAT-infested minds. When it comes to small churches, the truth according to Christ consists of two things: First, he values each small church and what it has to offer as much as he valued the little boy and his loaves and fish. Second, he can take the loaves and fish each small church has to offer and do miraculous things with them to impact the community and the kingdom of God. However, small-church leaders must be willing to resist the BATS or purge the BATS, if there has already been a BATS invasion.

Learn from the Little Boy

The best way to resist or purge the BATS is to learn from this little boy, whom Andrew viewed as insignificant, and follow him as a role model. We don't see the little boy again in Scripture, but what an impact he made! Jesus said, "Truly I tell you, unless you change and become like little children, you will never enter the kingdom of heaven" (Matt. 18:3). In context, Christ is speaking of the disciples' question about who is the greatest in the kingdom of heaven. However, it is important to note that the little boy with his loaves and fish manifested the humility that Christ points to in Matthew 18. In this place of humility, the little boy did three things:

- He recognized what he had.
- He told others (disciples) and shared what he had.
- In childlike faith, he gave it to Jesus and left the results to him.

The boy believed that his offering was significant when placed in the hands of Christ. Because of his humble belief, he witnessed Christ make a lasting impact on the lives of those who ate and on the lives of those who witnessed the miracle. The story concludes with the disciples gathering twelve baskets full of leftovers, and "after the people saw the sign Jesus performed, they began to say, 'Surely this is the Prophet who is to come into the world'" (John 6:14). And it all started with one little boy, free of BATS.

SMALL CHURCH, BIG IMPACT

Likewise, God can work in and through small churches to bring about a realization that he is using a church that the world may view as insignificant to convince the lost that Christ is the Messiah who has come to save them. Small-church leaders simply need to follow the little boy's example and recognize the loaves and fish the Lord has provided them, tell others, share what they have, and give the results to Jesus.

Recognize What You Have

Every small church has loaves and fish. As the Lord provided loaves and fish for the little boy to offer in a time of need, so he provides every small church, regardless of size, with loaves and fish. However, small-church pastors and lay leaders need to tune their minds to the mind of Christ to determine what those loaves and fish are and how he wants to use them to make an impact on his kingdom. As mentioned in chapter 1, one of the temptations that can lead to exhaustion, and perhaps burnout, is the urge to "run off in all directions," doing multiple things to stimulate growth that might or might not be in alignment with the loaves and fish the Lord has provided. In Matthew 11:30, Jesus states, "My yoke is easy and my burden is light." Whatever you determine your church should be doing for outreach, when centered in the heart and will of the Father, it will be doable, anointed, and natural for your church people, and chances are high that nobody will get burned out.

I recently spoke at a district small-church event, and a woman had a wonderful idea specific to her small church. I believe her idea is a good example of the mind of Christ engaging her mind to reveal some loaves and fish that he had provided her church. She said, "This idea is out of the box, but several people in our church own chickens, so we have eggs. We could get a stamp with our church's name, stamp the eggs, and give them out to our neighbors as an outreach effort." She spoke of buying the egg cartons that hold six eggs, rather than twelve, so the outreach effort could go farther. At the time this conversation took place, eggs were expensive, so we discussed how glad anyone would be to receive something of such high value in a market with overpriced eggs.

Eventually, I stated, "Those eggs are your small church's loaves and fish. And it sounds like the Lord is showing you exactly how you can use them for his kingdom."

As already related, when the idea came to the woman, she thought it was out of the box. For me, the out-of-the-box description is a strong indicator that the idea came straight from Christ because his whole life and ministry were out of the box. There is nothing more out of the box than Jesus taking five barley loaves and two fish and feeding five thousand-plus people. Tuning your mind to the mind of Christ may very well result in some out-of-the-box ideas because, well, Jesus just doesn't operate in the box. Why should he? He has the power to perform miracles! And he wants to work miracles with your church's loaves and fish. Remember, it's a miracle worth more than silver or gold when one soul experiences full salvation and deliverance from sin.

These loaves and fish the Lord has generously provided are like spiritual gold nuggets that small churches can give to others for an eternal impact. Perhaps your church's loaves and fish are as tangible as an egg you can hold in your hand. Perhaps your loaves and fish are a service your church provides, such as an after-school tutoring program staffed by volunteer retired schoolteachers who are church members. Perhaps your loaves and fish are a strength your church manifests, such as a powerful prayer ministry that draws people in as they lay their problems on the altar, surrounded by a group of loving and prayerful church members. The Lord may show you that your church has something tangible and something intangible to use for outreach. After all, the little boy didn't have just loaves *or* just fish; the Lord had given him both loaves *and* fish—two different things. Be open and attentive to what the Lord shows you, and don't be surprised if your loaves and fish lay outside the box.

The key is for small-church pastors and lay leaders to take their time and work collaboratively (see chap. 5) to allow the Lord to show them the loaves and fish he has placed at their fingertips. It's important to break away from telling attendees to follow what the leadership has already decided. Involve as many people as possible. Be creative together. People will get behind what they have helped develop.

Since every small church does not have members with chickens, every church cannot start an egg ministry. One church's loaves and fish are not going to be the same as another church's. It's important to move beyond trying to replicate what another church has done. Arbitrarily mimicking another church may blind church leaders from seeing their own loaves and fish. Furthermore, if the small church doesn't have a genuine strength to contribute to the replicated idea, then failure is more likely, which can lead to a defeated spirit, which, in turn, can lead to BATS. Therefore, it's important for a small church's pastor and lay leaders to allow the Lord to show them what will work in their specific context. This is not to say that copying another church's idea won't ever work. If your church has chicken owners who are seeing a vision on an egg ministry, then start stamping some eggs! However, it is important to invest some time and prayer into considering what the Lord shows you are *your* church's loaves and fish.

Tell Others What You Have and Share It

Once you have determined what your church's loaves and fish are, it's time to take the little boy's next step, telling others and sharing. Even though the text doesn't specifically state that the little boy told the disciples what he had, there is room for considering that this may be exactly what he did. For church participants, telling others and sharing may generate some excitement. It's the invigorating task of reaching others for the kingdom to give back to Jesus what he has given to us. Some people will find that sharing the loaves and fish is like a big adventure, and they will jump to the task with great enthusiasm.

However, there may be those who have fallen into the pit of fear and are thus hesitant to share their church's loaves and fish. Unfortunately, fear can propel the betrayal of loyalty, truth, or God's leading. We can live fearfully or faithfully, but not both. Even though Scripture states, "For God has not given us a spirit of fear, but of power and of love and of a sound mind" (2 Tim. 1:7, NKJV), so many church members are chained in the pit of fear about all sorts of things, including sharing their faith or inviting people to church. However, the fearful seldom come out and say they are fearful; that wouldn't sound very, well, spiritual. So the fearful may say, "Giving eggs to my neighbors is outside my comfort zone. They don't know me. They might slam the door in my face." First, if you do plan an outreach where you are providing something to eat in the current North American culture, you may want to begin by developing a positive acquaintance with someone before just showing up at his or her front door with a carton of eggs. Nevertheless, some people might even say, "It's out of my comfort zone to get acquainted with my neighbors," or "It just doesn't fit my personality type."

As already mentioned, Jesus is well known for operating outside of the box—and outside the fear pit. Unfortunately, there is nowhere in Scripture that suggests he is interested in leaving us chained in fear, keeping us in our boxes or comfort zones, or excusing certain personality types from reaching the lost. Quite the contrary, the New Testament is full of examples of Christ asking people to operate outside the box and step out of their comfort zones, such as when he called the disciples to leave the comfort of their livelihoods to follow him. Therefore, I can promise you, Jesus may very likely take your church leadership and attendees out of their comfort zones when it comes to telling others about your loaves and fish and sharing them.

In other words, God's goal is not to keep us in our comfort zones; his goal is to expand his kingdom and to use us to do it. And the Lord will give your church leaders and attendees the power to do exactly that through his Holy Spirit. Acts 1:8 promises us that this power is readily available for us to participate with him in expanding the kingdom of God: "But you will receive power when the Holy Spirit comes on you; and you will be my witnesses in Jerusalem, and in all Judea and Samaria [and wherever you share your loaves and fish], and to the ends of the earth." When sharing loaves and fish, you don't have to work in your own power, regardless of personality type or comfort zone. There is a power much greater than your own that will fill you and be the fuel that will impact the community surrounding your small church or your home, wherever your target outreach area may lie.

Imagine how the story of Jesus feeding the multitude would have changed if the little boy had hidden away in fear and hadn't stepped forward with his loaves and fish. Clearly, Jesus may have found some loaves and fish from someone else. Nevertheless, the little boy would not have had the joy and blessing of watching *his* loaves and fish being miraculously multiplied. The thing to remember is that the Lord is "not willing that any should perish but that all should come to repentance" (2 Pet. 3:9, NKJV), and he will work with us or without us to woo people to himself. When we fearfully clutch our loaves and fish, stay in our comfort zones, and, perhaps, use our personality types as an excuse not to participate with Christ, we also miss the opportunity to see him take our loaves and fish and work miracles in the lives of people in our community. We miss the blessing of a lifetime!

Give It to Jesus and Leave the Results with Him

A strong lay leader had watched his church decline from attendance in the four hundreds in the early 1960s to an average in the two hundreds by the early 1970s. In the early 1960s, the church had a vibrant radio ministry and a citywide outreach. The lay leader was grieved over the church's decline and the lack of people coming to know the Lord. So the Lord prompted him to give his retirement/life savings to the church for the purpose of evangelism. The devout churchman's life savings was $10,000, which was a significant amount of money in the early 1970s. When considering the impact of inflation, the current value of this layman's savings in today's market would be nearly $80,000. The layman's son recounts the meeting his father called with the family to explain his decision to donate his entire savings for the purpose of evangelism:

I remember him talking about it with the family, explaining what the Lord had asked him to do. I think he felt a sense of obligation that the family would know the plan in case something bad happened and he would have nothing in reserve. That's the only reason I even knew about the gift. I remember feeling a bit nervous that my dad had just given away our security net.

The church didn't initially know how to use the money, so it sat in the church's bank account for over ten years, providing a good example of some loaves and fish that were left unused. During those years, the church board approached the devout layman a few times, asking if he would allow them to use the ten grand for other purposes, such as building needs. However, the layman always said something to the effect that "the money was not given to be used for bricks and mortar, but for the saving of souls." So the money continued to sit in the bank, untapped, because, according to law, money designated for a particular purpose must be used for that purpose.

As the years rocked on, the church went through some conflicts and trauma and continued to decline. By the mid-1980s, the church that had once averaged four hundred-plus in attendance, now averaged in the eighties. And the $10,000 still sat in the church treasury, unused for evangelism.

Finally, the pastor at the time, not knowing what else to do, asked a young layman if he would let himself be hired as the church's evangelism coordinator. The $10,000 would be used to pay the young man's salary as he focused on evangelizing the community for Christ. The young man, grappling with a call to ministry, agreed to the task. He then spent months knocking on over two thousand doors in that community, with only one convert to show for the whole effort. However, the evangelism coordinator now reflects that "although only one convert emerged from the door knocking, it seems like the emphasis on evangelism pleased the Lord and altered the culture of the church because it doubled in the next few years to 170."

Through the process, the young man also solidified his call to ministry. God used the faithful layman's loaves and fish not only to reach a soul but also to confirm to this young man that he should commit his life to ministry. It would be very easy to think, *Just one convert?! That's all? That's not very impressive and not a great return on the money. Even in today's culture, ten grand is eighty grand, and that's a lot of money spent to show a return of only one soul.* But that one soul was worth way more than $10,000 or $80,000 to Christ because Christ gave his life for that soul. Furthermore, there was more involved in the process of evangelism than evangelism alone. The impact of committing to evangelism revolutionized the life of the young man who was hired for the purpose.

For you see, that young man who knocked on two thousand doors was Dr. Stan Reeder, former pastor and district superintendent and my denomination's current regional director for the United States and Canada. The devout layman who gave his life's savings to evangelism was Wesley Reeder, Dr. Reeder's father. The church was Hamilton First Church of the Nazarene, in Hamilton, Ontario, Canada, which continues as a solid church today.

Wesley Reeder had no way of knowing when he donated his life savings that his own son, then a preteen, would one day be the recipient of a ministry salary from those savings and that God would use his donation to solidify his son's call to ministry. He simply gave what he had—his loaves and fish—and left the results in the hands of the Lord. Furthermore, the son, who was nervous about his father giving away their family's financial security blanket, never imagined that the money would be used to provide financial security for him as he committed his time to the things of God. Speaking as a parent, I am convinced that the return Mr. Reeder saw for his life savings was worth way more to him than $10,000 or even $80,000, for there is no price too great for the eternal impact of one soul won and one soul called.

Speaking of his father, Dr. Stan Reeder further states, "He made a number of sacrificial gifts throughout his life, yet in the Lord's faithfulness, what was given away was always replenished. My dad's favorite verse was Proverbs 11:25*b* (KJV), 'He that watereth shall himself be watered.'"[2]

The little boy in John 6 did exactly what Wesley Reeder did. Once he told the disciples about his loaves and fish and shared his offering, he released it to Christ and let him work in his time. Fortunately, the little boy saw instant results that had to have inspired an instant blessing. However, when church leaders relinquish their loaves and fish, they may not always see instant results. Mr. Reeder had to wait over ten years to see the results of his sacrificial gift. I must wonder if he experienced times of frustration over his life savings just sitting in the church's bank account, not being used for what the Lord told him it should be used for. However, the Lord had his plan and his timing. Mr. Reeder's part was just to release his loaves and fish and leave them with the Lord.

Likewise, when small churches determine what their loaves and fish are, tell others, and share the loaves and fish, the last step is to release them to the Lord and let him use them to his glory in his time. It might be that your church will distribute what seems like ten thousand eggs (or cookies) to the community before seeing one person show an interest in salvation or church attendance. But that one person might be someone like

Dr. Stan Reeder, whom God will use in a prominent church leadership role. You just never know what Jesus has planned. It's our job to trust him and, in childlike faith, give our loaves and fish to him and leave the results in his hands.

The pit that is easy to fall into and that we must avoid is impatience and frustration when we don't see instant results from all our efforts. We must not forget that the Lord's timing is not our timing; his ways are not our ways. The multiplying is Christ's business, in his time, in his way. When we shift focus from the effort of reaching our community for the purpose of salvation to how we can make the numbers bigger in our church, we have shifted focus from the heart of Christ. Sharing the loaves and fish is not about numbers. It's about leading people to Christ and helping them put down deep, lasting spiritual roots.

"For we are God's fellow workers" (1 Cor. 3:9, NKJV).

The power of a small church is not found in great numbers, but in a great God and the loaves and fish he has provided that church. Whether a church has an attendance of five, fifty, or eighty-five, each person present is important to God. And God can empower each person to influence his or her community for him—one soul at a time. Small-church pastors and lay leaders simply need to avoid the pit of BATS the disciples were trapped in and claim the faith and victory the little boy walked in. Small churches need to refuse to cave to fear, and they must tell others about their loaves and fish, share them in Christlike faith, and give the results to Jesus to work his miracles.

PAUSING TO PLAN

- Each participant should choose at least one key concept he or she found especially meaningful or applicable to your church. As a group, discuss all the key concepts each participant has chosen.
- Does our small church have BATS? If yes, what steps do we need to take to remove the BATS?
- What are our church's "loaves and fish"? Brainstorm and list everything that comes to mind.
- How can we use our "loaves and fish" to minister to our community?
- This chapter identified comfort-zone issues as a hindrance to sharing "loaves and fish." Do we have comfort-zone issues that can hinder our efforts? If yes, what are they and what steps do we need to take to overcome the issues?

Afterword
Implementing the Plan

●────────────●

Victory is won through many advisers.

—Prov. 11:14

My vision for this book is to help pastors and lay leaders work together to bring about a lasting and sustainable difference in their churches that will result in church growth in all areas, including the evangelism of souls for Christ. However, the plan must be reasonable and doable. An overachieving plan that has numerous people "running off in all directions" will fizzle. A good plan is one that is set in motion at a moderate pace and that fits the church's current time and resource capacities. It will not be completed overnight. It must be implemented over time. Furthermore, a solid plan will have a "loop effect" so that parts of the plan will operate perpetually and thus continue to circle back to the salvation of sinners and the consecration of believers to live the sanctified life. Such a plan will never be fully completed, because the need for the salvation and sanctification of souls never ends.

With that said, if all has gone as intended as you worked through this book, your church leadership team—pastor and lay leaders—should have developed a doable plan that is specific to your church. Now comes the important part of organizing and applying the plan. As you prayerfully consider your plan, allow the Lord to direct you to what order you should implement the items in your plan. Your church may have just experienced a season of Spirit-filled revival that renewed the church's spiritual and relational health, so you can proceed to implement the numerical growth part of your plan while also applying as needed its relational and spiritual elements. On the other hand, your church may not be as healthy spiritually as it needs to be. If that is the case, you will need to focus on the spiritual growth and commitment of attendees. The Lord may lead you to focus on the spiritual growth of attendees for months before moving to another segment of growth. Your church may be facing some of the challenges the last two chapters speak to, and those challenges need to be resolved or placed into balance as one of the first elements in your plan. Finally, teaching about the effects of the consumer culture should be woven into each church's plan and should be an ongoing process. The only way we can see victory over the consumer culture is if attendees are trained to see the consumer culture, to recognize its impact, and to learn to tune their hearts to hearing the Lord, rather than the voice of consumerism. Each church has its own needs, based on its specific setting. Ask the Lord to guide you as you proceed with your plan.

One further thing to keep in mind is that after a plan is developed, often the commitment to the plan fades and old patterns resume with no real changes going forward. Hence, the following suggestions should assist with maintaining the focus on applying the plan:

- **Review the plan as part of your regular board meetings.** The leadership team should be honest about their adherence to the plan and any needed improvement in implementing and following the plan. Don't be surprised if there are times you look at each other and say, "We aren't following through the way we need to." Admitting the need for improvement is healthy and will lead to the needed plan application. The board meeting can also be the time the plan is adjusted based on what is working and what is not working. Don't hesitate to adjust the plan as needed. The plan should work and grow with your church, and if one element doesn't fit your church, that doesn't mean the whole process is faulty or the whole plan is wrong. Make the changes and move forward with the plan. Remember, a good plan is in place to serve your church; your church should not serve the plan.
- **Find a partner church and hold each other accountable for following the plan.** The pastors can have a monthly phone call to report to each other how they are doing with their plans. The lay leaders and pastors can meet in person or via Zoom two to four times a year just to dialogue together and discuss how their plans are going. The pastors and lay leaders may also share ideas so they can help each other reach their communities.
- **Meet several times a year with a small-church coach in person or via Zoom.** Share your plan with the coach and work with him or her to keep your church on target in applying the plan. The Revitalization Network (www .therevitalization.net) offers church coaching specifically for small churches.

Taken together, these suggestions illustrate an important point: you need a plan for the plan. Without a support plan for the church growth plan, there is a higher chance that the church growth plan will remain as nothing more than words on paper. Therefore, remaining actively determined to adhere to the plan and to adjust it as needed is paramount to the plan's success.

As you move forward, please know that I will be regularly praying for each pastor and lay leader who reads this book, and that means *you*. I don't know you by name, but the Lord does. My prayer is that the Lord will powerfully move in your life, in your ministry, and in your small church to do great things for his kingdom at an hour in our culture when a mighty movement of God is desperately needed. There is an echo across the land that God is moving and wants to use small churches to evangelize North America. I fully believe that he can and will move in your small church for the purpose of leading people to our Lord and Savior, Jesus Christ. To God be the Glory!

Notes

Preface

1. Church of the Nazarene, "Church Size Categories," 2022, www.naz areneresearch.com.

2. Stan Reeder, personal communication, October 25, 2022.

3. Reeder.

4. Justin Nortey and Michael Rotolo, "How the Pandemic Has Affected Attendance at U.S. Religious Services," Pew Research Center, March 28, 2023, https://www.pewresearch.org/religion/2023/03/28/how-the-pandemic -has-affected-attendance-at-u-s-religious-services/.

5. Jeffrey M. Jones, "U.S. Church Membership Down Sharply in Past Two Decades," GALLUP, April 18, 2019, https://news.gallup.com /poll/248837/church-membership-down-sharply-past-two-decades.aspx.

6. "Size of Congregation," Association of Religion Data Archives, 2012, accessed August 10, 2019, http://www.thearda.com/ConQS/qs_295.asp.

7. Debra White Smith, "Ministerial Training on Consumer Culture and Volunteer Management May Prevent Burnout for Small-Church Clergy," *Pastoral Psychology* 69, no. 3 (June 2020): 225-48, https://link.springer.com /article/10.1007/s11089-020-00905-6.

Chapter 1

1. Aaron B. James, "Rehabilitating Willow Creek: Megachurches, De Certeau, and the Tactics of Navigating Consumer Culture," *Christian Scholar's Review* 43, no. 1 (October 15, 2013): 30, https://christianscholars.com /rehabilitating-willow-creek-megachurches-de-certeau-and-the-tactics -of-navigating-consumer-culture/.

2. Sue C. Jansen, "Semantic Tyranny: How Edward L. Bernays Stole Walter Lippmann's Mojo and Got Away with It and Why It Still Matters," *International Journal of Communication* 7, (2013): 1094-1111, https://ijoc .org/index.php/ijoc/article/view/1955/907.

3. Iris Mostegel, "The Great Manipulator," *History Today* 66, no. 1 (January 2016): 41-45.

4. Vanessa Murphree, "Edward Bernays's 1929 'Torches of Freedom' March: Myths and Historical Significance," *American Journalism* 32, no. 3 (2015): 258-81, https://doi.org/10.1080/08821127.2015.1064681.

5. Jansen, "Semantic Tyranny."

6. Mostegel, "Great Manipulator."

7. Murphree, "'Torches of Freedom' March."

8. Jansen, "Semantic Tyranny."

9. Mostegel, "Great Manipulator."

10. Murphree, "'Torches of Freedom' March."

11. Murphree.

12. "Edward Bernays and Why We Eat Bacon for Breakfast," Braithwaite Communications, accessed August 20, 2024, https://gobraithwaite.com /thinking/edward-bernays-and-why-we-eat-bacon-for-breakfast/.

13. Robert F. Cartwright and Suzanna J. Opree, "All That Glitters Is Not Gold: Do Materialistic Cues in Advertising Yield Resistance?" *Young Consumers* 17, no. 2 (2016): 183-96, https://doi.org/10.1108/YC-12-2015 -00573.

14. Ryan LaMothe, "Broken and Empty: Pastoral Leadership as Embodying Radical Courage, Humility, Compassion, and Hope," *Pastoral Psychology* 61, no. 4 (2012): 451-66, https://doi.org/10.1007/s11089-011-0417-9.

15. William C. Martin and Connie R. Bateman, "Consumer Religious Commitment's Influence on Ecocentric Attitudes and Behavior," *Journal of Business Research* 67, no. 2 (February 2014): 5-11, https://doi.org/10.1016/j .jbusres.2013.03.006.

16. Lynn Metcalf et al., "A Mixed-Methods Approach for Designing Market-Driven Packaging," *Qualitative Market Research* 15, no. 3 (2012): 268-89, https://doi.org/10.1108/13522751211231987.

17. Andrew Rohm, Velitchka D. Kaltcheva, and George R. Milne, "A Mixed-Method Approach to Examining Brand-Consumer Interactions

Driven by Social Media," *Journal of Research in Interactive Marketing* 7, no. 4 (2013): 295-311, https://doi.org/10.1108/JRIM-01-2013-0009.

18. Timothy M. Brunk, "Consumer Culture and Sacramental Reconciliation," *Worship* 92, no. 4 (July 2018): 337-60.

19. Riza Casidy, "How Great Thy Brand: The Impact of Church Branding on Perceived Benefits," *International Journal of Nonprofit and Voluntary Sector Marketing* 18, no. 3 (2013): 231-39, http://doi.org/10.1002/nvsm.1467.

20. Florin C. Dobocan, "Antecedents of the Loyalty of Religious Service Consumers," *International Conference "Marketing—from Information to Decision"* 7 (2014): 81-90, https://www.ceeol.com/search/article-detail?id=48806.

21. Metcalf et al., "Designing Market-Driven Packaging."

22. Durdana Ozretic-Dosen, Marta Brlic, and Tanja Komarac, "Strategic Brand Management in Emerging Markets: Consumer Perceptions of Brand Extensions," *Organizations and Markets in Emerging Economies* 9, no. 1 (2018): 135-53, https://doi.org/10.15388/omee.2018.10.00008.

23. Casidy, "How Great Thy Brand."

24. Dobocan, "Loyalty of Religious Service Consumers."

25. James, "Rehabilitating Willow Creek."

26. C. Zech, W. Wagner, and R. West, "The Effective Design of Church Web Sites: Extending the Consumer Evaluation of Web Sites to the Non-Profit Sector," *Information Systems Management* 30, no. 2 (2013): 92-99, https://doi.org/10.1080/10580530.2013.773800.

27. Casidy, "How Great Thy Brand."

28. Dobocan, "Loyalty of Religious Service Consumers."

29. James, "Rehabilitating Willow Creek."

30. Zech, Wagner, and West, "Design of Church Web Sites."

31. Smith, "Ministerial Training on Consumer Culture."

Chapter 2

1. Joel Comiskey, "What Was the New Testament Church Like?" Smallgroups.com, *Christianity Today*, 2015, https://www.smallgroups.com/articles/2015/what-was-new-testament-church-like.html.

2. Joel Comiskey, "Women in the History of Small Groups," Smallgroups.com, *Christianity Today*, 2015, https://www.smallgroups.com/articles/2015/women-in-history-of-small-groups.html.

3. Sheila Thompson (pastor), personal communication, June 2023.

4. Karl Vaters, "The Astonishing Power of Small Churches: Over One Billion Served," KarlVaters.com, February 4, 2013, https://karlvaters.com/the-astonishing-power-of-small-churches-over-one-billion-served/.

5. Church of the Nazarene, "Church Size Categories," 2022, received from Rich Houseal, email message to author, October 9, 2023.

6. Church of the Nazarene, "Church Size Categories," 2016, received from Rich Houseal, email message to author, February 10, 2017.

7. "Size of Congregation," Association of Religion Data Archives, 2012, accessed August 10, 2019, http://www.thearda.com/ConQS/qs_295.asp.

8. Stan Reeder, personal communication, November 3, 2023.

9. Vaters, "Over One Billion Served."

10. Jason Helopoulos, "Kids Worshiping: Why Children Should Attend the Adult Service," ChurchLeaders.com, February 22, 2023, https://churchleaders.com/children/childrens-ministry-articles/308187-let-children-worship-church-jason-helopoulos.html.

11. Beth Bidle Rush, EdD ABD, personal communication, December 22, 2023.

12. Gary Portnoy and Judy Hart-Angelo, "Where Everybody Knows Your Name (Theme from Cheers)," Lyrics.com, STANDS4 LLC, accessed August 22, 2024, https://www.lyrics.com/lyric-lf/1565392/The+Wedding+Present/Where+Everybody+Knows+Your+Name+%28Theme+from+Cheers%29.

13. Comiskey, "New Testament Church."

Chapter 3

1. Haldor Lillenas, "My Wonderful Lord," in *Sing to the Lord* (Kansas City: Lillenas, 1993), no. 111.

2. For more information on entire sanctification, see "Articles of Faith," in *Manual, Church of the Nazarene, 2023* (Kansas City: Nazarene Publishing House, 2023), paras. 1-16, esp. para. 10.

Chapter 4

1. Karl Vaters, "The Astonishing Power of Small Churches: Looking Ahead," KarlVaters.com, February 8, 2013, https://karlvaters.com/the-astonishing-power-of-small-churches-looking-ahead/.

2. Scott Rainey (former global director of Nazarene Discipleship International), personal communication, June 2023.

Chapter 5

1. Anne T. Fraker and Larry C. Spears, preface to *Seeker and Servant: Reflections on Religious Leadership: The Private Writings of Robert K. Greenleaf*, ed. A. T. Fraker and L. C. Spears (San Francisco: Jossey-Bass, 1996).

2. "Robert K. Greenleaf," Robert K. Greenleaf Center for Servant Leadership, accessed August 23, 2024, https://www.greenleaf.org/robert-k-greenleaf-biography/#.

3. Robert K. Greenleaf, *The Servant as Leader*, rev. ed. (Westfield, IN: Greenleaf Center for Servant Leadership, 2008).

4. Greenleaf.

5. Greenleaf.

6. Hermann Hesse, *The Journey to the East* (New York: Noonday Press, 1956).

7. Greenleaf, *Servant as Leader*.

8. Robert K. Greenleaf, *Servant Leadership: A Journey into the Nature of Legitimate Power and Greatness*, 25th anniv. ed. (Mahwah, NJ: Paulist Press, 2002).

Chapter 6

1. Holley Collier, personal communication, 2020.

2. Rob Beckett (pastor), personal communication, February 17, 2024.

3. David Craig (pastor), personal communication, November 14, 2023.

4. Craig.

Chapter 7

1. Janet Eccles, "Older English Churchgoing Women as Voluntary Providers of Welfare," *Journal of Beliefs and Values* 35, no. 3 (2014): 315-26, https://doi.org/10.1080/13617672.2014.980072.

2. Paul Vermeer, Peer Scheepers, and Manfred te Grotenhuis, "Churches: Lasting Sources of Civic Engagement? Effects of Secularization and Educational Expansion on Non-religious Volunteering in the Netherlands, 1988 and 2006," *Voluntas* 27, no. 3 (2016): 1361-84, https://doi.org/10.1007/s11266-016-9679-2.

3. Eccles, "Older English Churchgoing Women."

4. Karen Granger et al., "Keeping the Faith! Drivers of Participation in Spiritually Based Communities," *Journal of Business Research* 67, no. 2 (2014): 68-75, https://doi.org/10.1016/j.jbusres.2013.03.013.

5. Vermeer, Scheepers, and Grotenhuis, "Churches."

6. James, "Rehabilitating Willow Creek," 21-39.

7. Thomas White and Jon M. Yeats, *Franchising McChurch: Feeding Our Obsession with Easy Christianity* (Colorado Springs: David C. Cook, 2009), Kindle.

8. Justine B. Allen and Mike Bartle, "Sport Event Volunteers' Engagement: Management Matters," *Managing Leisure* 19, no. 1 (2014): 36-50, https://doi.org/10.1080/13606719.2013.849502.

9. Mark A. Hager and Jeffrey L. Brudney, "In Search of Strategy: Universalistic, Contingent, and Configurational Adoption of Volunteer Management Practices," *Nonprofit Management and Leadership* 25, no. 3 (2015): 235-54, https://doi.org/10.1002/nml.21123.

10. Pietra Borchardt and Mônica de Fátima Bianco, "Meanings of Volunteer Work: A Study with Members of a Lutheran Institution," *MacKenzie Management Review* 17, no. 5 (2016): 61-84, http://dx.doi.org/10.1590/1678 -69712016/administracao.v17n5p61-84.

11. Loise Waikayi et al., "Volunteer Management: An Exploratory Case Study within the British Red Cross," *Management Decision* 50, no. 3 (2012): 349-67, https://doi.org/10.1108/00251741211216188.

12. Borchardt and Bianco, "Meanings of Volunteer Work."

13. Daniel Curtis, Ram A. Cnaan, and Van Evans, "Motivating Mormons: An Analysis of What Motivates Members of the Church of Jesus Christ of Latter-Day Saints to Volunteer and Donate," *Nonprofit Management and Leadership* 25, no. 2 (2014): 131-45, https://doi.org/10.1002 /nml.21113.

14. Borchardt and Bianco, "Meanings of Volunteer Work."

15. Yi-Jung Liu, "Long-Term Care Residents' Views about the Contributions of Christian-Based Volunteers in Taiwan: A Pilot Study," *Journal of Religion and Health* 51, no. 3 (2012): 709-22, https://doi.org/10.1007 /s10943-010-9339-6.

16. Waikayi et al., "Volunteer Management."

17. Smith, "Ministerial Training on Consumer Culture."

18. Leslie J. Francis, Peter Hills, and Peter Kaldor, "The Oswald Clergy Burnout Scale: Reliability, Factor Structure and Preliminary Application among Australian Clergy," *Pastoral Psychology* 57, nos. 5-6 (2009): 243-52, https://doi.org/10.1007/s11089-008-0165-7.

Chapter 8

1. Robert Burns, "To a Louse, on Seeing One on a Lady's Bonnet at Church" (1786), "To a Louse," Wikipedia, Wikimedia Foundation, last modified July 18, 2024, 17:13 (UTC), https://en.wikipedia.org/wiki/To_a _Louse.

2. Stan Reeder, personal communication, November 3, 2023.

www.ingramcontent.com/pod-product-compliance
Lightning Source LLC
Chambersburg PA
CBHW051419090426
42737CB00014B/2748